FIRST
COMES
LOVE

ALSO BY MARION WINIK

Telling

FIRST
COMES
LOVE

MARION WINIK

PANTHEON BOOKS

NEW YORK

Copyright © 1996 by Marion Winik

A portion of this work was originally published in *American Way* Magazine.

Grateful acknowledgment is made to the following for permission to reprint previously published material: BMG Music Publishing: Excerpt from "Miracle of Love" by Annie Lennox and David Stewart, copyright © 1986 by D'N'A Limited. All rights for the world controlled by BMG Music Publishing LTD. All rights for the USA controlled by Careers-BMG Music Publishing, Inc. (BMI). Reprinted by permission of BMG Music Publishing. • *Cherry Lane Music Publishing Company, Inc.:* Excerpts from "Once Upon a Dream" by Leslie Bricusse and Frank Wildhorn, copyright © 1990 by Stage and Screen Music, Ltd. (BMI)/Les Étoiles De La Musique (ASCAP)/Scaramanga Music, Inc. (ASCAP)/Cherry Lane Music Publishing Company, Inc. (ASCAP). Worldwide rights for Stage and Screen Music, Ltd. administered by Cherry River Music Co. (BMI). Worldwide rights for Les Étoiles De La Musique and Scaramanga Music, Inc., administered by Cherry Lane Music Publishing Company (ASCAP). All rights reserved. Reprinted by permission of Cherry Lane Music Publishing Company, Inc. • *The Famous Music Publishing Companies:* Excerpt from "Up Where We Belong" by Will Jennings, Buffy Sainte-Marie, and Jack Nitzsche, copyright © 1982 by Famous Music Corporation and Ensign Music Corporation. Reprinted by permission of The Famous Music Publishing Companies. • *Hal Leonard Corporation:* Excerpt from "Sign Your Name" by Terence Trent D'Arby, copyright © 1987 by EMI Virgin Music Ltd. All rights controlled and administered by EMI Virgin Songs, Inc. (BMI). All rights reserved. International copyright secured. Reprinted by permission of Hal Leonard Corporation. • *Sequins At Noon Music and Blue Image Music:* Excerpt from "Do Ya Wanna Funk?" by Sylvester James and Patrick Cowley. Reprinted by permission of Sequins At Noon Music (BMI) and Blue Image Music (PRO).

Library of Congress Cataloging-in-Publication Data

Winik, Marion.
First comes love / Marion Winik.
p.   cm.
ISBN 0-679-44572-2
1. Winik, Marion.
2. AIDS (Disease)—Patients—Family relationships.
3. Married people—United States—Biography.   I. Title.
RC607.A26W574   1996
362.1'969792'0092—dc20
[B]   95-42674
                                                              CIP

Book design by Maura Fadden Rosenthal
Manufactured in the United States of America
First Edition
2   4   6   8   9   7   5   3   1

for Tony

Having observed that I have all my life acted more from the force of feeling than from my reflections, I have concluded that my conduct has depended more on my character than on my mind, after a long struggle in which I have alternately found myself with too little intelligence for my character and too little character for my intelligence.

—GIACOMO CASANOVA, *History of My Life*

FIRST
COMES
LOVE

TONY SLEEPING

Tony has never looked more beautiful than he does right now, sleeping, his features sculpted and glowing by the light of the candles. They are the Mexican kind, in tall glasses, two white and two blue as he requested, arranged in a semicircle around our wedding photograph: my gauzy veil, his spiky hair, our wide, giddy smiles. Under the edge of the picture's vermilion frame, he has slipped another photo, a dreamy-looking sepia-tone postcard of a woman dancing that someone gave him on his birthday in the hospital last month; she seems only half there, as if she had turned the corner into another dimension.

On the lower shelf of the night table, there are two goblets of red wine, still full, along with Tony's rimless eyeglasses, which I just took off for him. The table is one of a pair he bought at an estate sale, then stripped and painted and drizzled with wavy lines of pink and white paint—a typical Tony home improvement project in that it took almost a year and he ran out of paint before he finished all the boomerang-shaped decks. Its twin stands on the other side of the bed, a firm and lovely king-size model that we acquired when I was pregnant with Vince and damned if I would go through another pregnancy on that old futon of ours. Flanked by these tables, the bed has always reminded me of the Starship *Enterprise,* about to take off for the final frontier.

I have been watching Tony sleep for almost twelve years, on and off, since the early days when I was so keyed up and hungry that at night I lay wide-eyed beside him, gazing at him, examining him, drinking and eating him with my eyes. In the morning, I would wake up first, make coffee, come back to bed to look some more. I filled sketchbooks with drawings of him sleeping. The dark lashes against the cheek, the long arm thrown out against the pillow, the fingers curled slightly toward the palm. Years later, I took a series of photographs of him napping with Hayes; in the first, a few days after Hayes's birth, they are sleeping on the lambskin baby spread together and there is that arm again, the baby no longer than the distance from wrist to elbow.

When you think how much of a person's beauty is in their eyes, it is astonishing how beautiful they can be with them closed in sleep, perhaps as when you suddenly notice how talented the members of a chorus line are once the stars of the show have left the stage. Finally, you can look at something else. His hair, for instance, cut the way I like it best, long in front, short at the sides and back. We call it the don't-ever-change do because he alternates between this and more extreme cuts, and whenever he returns to this look, my mother and her friends at the club say, Don't ever change. It is beautiful hair, thick and shiny, a sandy forelock jutting forward and slanting down almost into his eyes. He's been complaining of its falling out and changing texture from the medication, but I don't see it, only that the color didn't lighten this year because he didn't spend that much time outside. Normally, his hair bleaches almost blond every summer, the color it was when he was a boy, the color Hayes's and Vince's is now.

The boys look so much like him, especially Hayes; I've seen a picture of Tony at nine, ice-skating on a pond, that could easily be our son. Hayes doesn't quite have the eyebrows yet, the thick, dark Italian brows Tony inherited from his mother. Beneath them, Tony's closed eyelids are shadowy and delicate, almost waxen, set deep in the rim of bone. The long planes of his cheeks are made of coarser stuff, less than smooth since the last shave, and I know just how they move, how they crease when he smiles, how they suck in when he smokes, how they work when he is angry, and all this is there in their stillness.

His nose is perfect, long but not too long, thin but not too thin, with a slight boyish lift at the tip, and some of this is thanks to the miracle of plastic surgery. When we met, our nose jobs were just another of the many amazing things we had in common. His was broken in a fight at a New Orleans movie theater years before I met him, over a parking space, I believe.

His mouth, wide and beautiful, deeply colored, the etched V of the upper lip and the sensual push of the lower over the clefted chin, lips I have kissed so many times and I am kissing them now, brushing them gently and then I can't keep my hand from fluttering over his shoulder, along his collarbone, inside his shirt, the soft hair on his flat chest and stomach, God he is so thin. He has always been slender, but now his bones have nothing to cushion them, they are jutting out everywhere, awkward and raw and painful to look at. Oh, the five thousand nights this body and I curled together against the cold and the dark, I want to pull him to me again, feel how the curve of his butt fits in the cup of my hips, my belly against the small of his back, my breasts against his shoulder blades, my leg slipped between his.

And I would lightly trace the slight curve down to the forest of black hair and his penis, do I dare touch it, it is heavy and somnolent, the thick weight of it curled over my palm, now I am remembering everything and I have to let go I am scaring myself should I call the doctor his breathing is thick and labored and I have to pull away, it is an action before it is a thought. The thought is to take a photograph, is that grotesque? I don't know I don't care it is too quiet between these difficult congested breaths quick take the picture then get out of here the boys' Polaroid is on the dresser and I am looking for the right angle I am barefoot standing on the end of the bed standing over him with a camera taking the last picture I will ever take of Tony and he is so beautiful, my poor sick angry dying junkie baby is so beautiful, released finally from his sickness and his anger and his junk and even his dying and he was so brave! so goddamn brave and calm and sure and clear, no self-pity, no fear, not a victim anymore. I felt it all day long. He was casual, smoking cigarettes, laughing a little, kvetching a little, still Tony, but he was walking straight toward someplace else without looking back. It was almost holy, it is holy now and takes away my unsureness and unclearness and worries about motives and power, right and wrong, and I see now this is his, this is his.

I am sitting on the edge of the bed, if I were not so numb my heart would be breaking, if it were not already broken my heart would be breaking, I am drinking the wine in big sips, the fancy red wine he wanted, and I am waiting for the Polaroid to develop. It is coming out with a greenish cast, not beautiful and rosy like he looks. The breathing is getting worse and worse and I am afraid to be here but I can't leave. Jesus Christ, Tony, did you really do this? Did I really let you? Are you really leaving?

Oh baby oh baby, I whisper, saying it to him and to myself, finally crying after the eerie calm of this whole long day, the chaos of this whole long week, this whole long month, these many years of everything that could never happen happening and happening, for better and worse, for breakfast and babies, for road trips and fistfights, till death, that stupid unthinkable, out in the corridor all along, comes in with his noisy vacuum cleaner to do us part.

FIRST SIGHT

When you drive into New Orleans on I-10 early in the morning, it takes a while to realize you have actually arrived. The city rises slowly from the swamps, wrapped in an old gray bathrobe of a morning sky, her suburbs sprawling around like grown children too lazy to leave home. Unlike cities that spring frantically into action at dawn, New Orleans seems to be waiting for breakfast in bed, her morning rush hour drenched in languor.

I had been in the car for thirty-two hours, driving for the last eight, speeding down the deserted interstate, feeling the truck-stop caffeine catch hold in my blood, seeing only the cone of light boring through the blackness ahead of me. My miasma of gloom had begun to lift. Now the sky was light and downtown lay ahead. The scents of car exhaust and bayou and doughnuts floated in on the chilly air like ghostly fingers in a cartoon, beckoning the muddled hero to adventure.

I followed Shelley's botanically detailed directions into town, off the highway and up St. Charles Avenue, a wide boulevard lined by antebellum mansions with wrought-iron gates, divided by the grassy track of the old-fashioned streetcar. I was supposed to turn left at a house with a big magnolia tree. Sandye, I said, nudging her. Wake up, honey. You gotta help me.

When Sandye, my best friend since elementary school and currently one of my roommates in New York, had suggested we drive down and visit our friends Shelley and Pete in New Orleans over Mardi Gras, I was unenthusiastic. I was in a serious year-long tailspin after a disastrous love affair and had become nearly addicted to heroin and misery in the process. At twenty-four, I had melodramatically decided my life was over, my prospects nonexistent. Leaving town would be pointless even if it was chemically feasible.

Sandye, however, was on a rescue mission and refused to take no for an answer. She had been down to Shelley and Pete's earlier that year and regaled me with descriptions of their funny little apartment in the Garden District, of Pete's gumbos and red beans and crawfish, of their friend Tony, the gorgeous gay ice-skater, who would give us free drinks at the bar he worked at in the French Quarter. It sounds like fun, I said vaguely, just to appease her.

The plan gathered momentum without me, however, and soon my sister Nancy and her boyfriend Steven, with whom we shared a pathetic fifth-floor walk-up in the no-man's-land between the West Village and Chelsea, were planning to fly down and join us. In the process of working on me, Sandye had managed to sign up one of my classmates from the MFA writing program at Brooklyn College, a woman I worked with at the Stanley H. Kaplan Educational Center, and a guy we met one night at a bar. On the appointed day, they all showed up and shoved me into the car. I don't think it even occurred to anyone that this rest cure they were dragging me off to was in fact one of the largest-scale public debauches in the civilized world.

I was not much of an asset the first three-quarters of the trip, having done a big farewell shot of dope before I left the house. Once it wore off, too much drugs, too little sleep, and dragging myself to work and to school every day caught up with me and I was comatose through many large central and southern states. Finally, around Birmingham, I woke up in the crowded backseat.

Let me drive for a while, I said, sliding forward so that the sleeping bodies on either side of me collapsed together.

All yours, said Sandye, ready for a nap herself.

She came instantly back to life when I woke her on St. Charles and, after using the rearview mirror to reapply her Frankly Fuchsia lipstick and refasten the many plastic barrettes in her black curly hair, she and my writing-program friend successfully identified not only a magnolia but a Japanese plum, a crape myrtle, and an azalea bush, leading us ultimately to our destination, a run-down Victorian mansion which had been converted to apartments, at the corner of Second and Chestnut. It was not yet 7 A.M. on Tuesday, February 8, 1983, when we did our clowns-from-a-Volkswagen routine in front of the house.

The door was answered by a tall, slender young man with honey-colored hair, clear brown eyes, and a long, arrestingly handsome face. Tony! Sandye cried, throwing her arms around him.

Welcome back, Miss Thing, he said, smiling over her head at the rest of us.

Shelley and Pete emerged from the shadows behind him in their faded T-shirts and messy hairdos. Neither was much taller than five feet, and next to Tony they looked shorter than that. They weren't big huggers, but seemed glad to see us in their don't-make-a-big-deal-out-of-it way.

The five of us, the three of them, and all our stuff gradually relocated from the front stoop into the one-room apartment, where a pot of chicory coffee, a case of generic beer, and a jar of Pete's famous pickled eggs awaited on a folding metal bridge table in the center of the combination bedroom/living room/dining room/recording studio/printmaking shop. Introductions were made, and we milled around the room eating and drinking for a while without saying much. Once the coffee kicked in, Shelley whipped out a parade schedule and started filling us in on Mardi Gras activities and customs. Her tiny figure, long, un-raveling red braids, granny glasses, and raggy clothes made her look like a porcelain music-box figurine on its day off.

I was trying to pay attention but found myself seriously dis-tracted by Tony, who was stretched out on Pete and Shelley's spartan, army-blanketed twin bed, reading the paper. He was still wearing his work outfit from an all-night shift at the bar—a white shirt with rolled-up sleeves, black jeans, and pointy-toed ankle boots.

I'll make another pot, Tony said as the last cup of coffee was poured, hopping up from the bed and going into the kitchen. When he came back, he sat at the table next to Shelley. The two of them started going over the parade listing more closely, trying to see what he could fit in around his work schedule.

Something about him was drawing me like a magnet. Maybe it was his East Coast way of talking—it turned out he'd grown up an hour and a half away from my New Jersey hometown, in a suburb north of Philadelphia—or maybe the wide, boyish smile that revealed his chipped front tooth. Whatever it was, after about fifteen minutes it became so intense I had to go sit in his lap. I didn't even think about it, I just did it.

Perhaps because we were all so overtired, my bold move didn't seem that outrageous at the time. There were only half as many chairs as people; why not double up? Tony accepted my ap-pearance on his knee with equanimity, stuffing a whole egg into my mouth.

Somebody's got to go out and get supplies for Bloody Marys, it was decided around 10:30 A.M. Tony volunteered, Sandye gave him her car keys, and I said I'd come along for the ride.

He turned on the black radio station, which was playing Michael Jackson's "Billie Jean," lit two cigarettes at once, then passed one to me. He was wearing gloves with the fingers cut off, dark glasses, and a black leather jacket. I was chattering giddily, as if we were on a date.

At the Canal Villere supermarket, I was amazed to see aisles of hard liquor right alongside the cereal and baloney and dishwashing liquid.

Oh, yeah, this town is Party World, Tony told me. You can buy liquor anywhere, anytime, you can drink on the street, some of the drugstores even have real drugs. You're going to love it here.

On the way out of the store, laden with vodka, V-8, horseradish, Tabasco, lemons, celery salt, and actual celery, all of which Tony required for what he assured me would be the ultimate Bloody Mary, I saw a display of Mardi Gras–brand beer, stacked high in gleaming gold, green, and purple cans.

Look! I said. Let's get some.

Good idea, Tony said as he picked up a case.

A case? I said. Isn't there a case back at the house?

I'm sure Noonie Bell and Pete and your friends have done that one in by now.

I assumed Noonie Bell was his name for Shelley. I wondered covetously if he would someday call me by a nickname too.

As we loaded our groceries into the car, Tony asked if, since this was my first visit to town, I wanted to do a little sightseeing, maybe drive out to the levee. I didn't even know what a levee was, except that it had been dry in the song "American Pie," but already I would have gone anywhere with him.

He pulled into a parking lot on the banks of the wide, gray Mississippi and reached into the backseat for some beers.

How long have you been living with Shelley and Pete? I asked him.

Since Larone threw me and my suitcase down the stairs, he said.

La-who?

Larone. My ex-boyfriend. The bitch.

Oh my God, I exclaimed, reaching for the dial of the radio.

What, you know him?

No, this song, I said excitedly. I had just heard the beginning notes of "Do Ya Wanna Funk?"

There is something I wanna ask you, I sang along with Sylvester, jumping up to stand on the seat to dance, my upper body sticking out of the open sunroof. *There is something that I want to know.*

A stupid question, you have the answer, so tell me what I want to know, Tony joined in. Like most disco songs, this one wasn't long on memorable lyrics, but it had the commanding, throbbing, about-to-explode sensuality that made it the music of choice for gay men, cokeheads, accountants, and other party people of the early eighties.

Do ya wanna funk? we both shouted. *Won't you tell me now? If you wanna funk let me show you how, do you wanna funk with me?*

When the song ended, it was all I could do not to throw my arms around him. If there was really such a thing as love at first sight, I thought I might very well be experiencing it with this half-elegant, half-goofy twenty-five-year-old Mario Anthony Heubach, whose combination of James Dean cool and genuine niceness I found wildly attractive. Weirdly, the fact that he was gay only increased the abandon with which I launched into all-out crush behavior. I had never been big on patience or self-control in the first place, and Tony's well-known preference for men seemed to make it that much easier to flirt outrageously, touch him casually, and instantly assume an easy, teasing friendship between us. It was a common enough way for a straight woman and a gay man to be together, though just as commonly there is a hidden agenda on the woman's part. Not very well hidden, in my case.

I don't think I am romanticizing to say there was some spark of recognition between Tony and me, something that went deeper than the encounter between our public personae—crazy romantic poetess and gay ice-skater. I had the sense that something unexpected was happening, something with a trajectory far outside my field of vision. Nothing could have pleased me more.

THREE FOR TWO

One of the first things Tony and I learned we had in common, after disco music, was drugs. Great. I had drugs to share. Actually, they were my sister Nancy's drugs, but she hadn't yet arrived from New York. Planning ahead, she had packaged up six bags of heroin, sixty dollars' worth, and sent them to herself in New Orleans, care of Shelley.

Me and Steve are taking three each, she told me. What do you want?

I told her not to put in any for me; I said it would do me good to take a week off. This was undoubtedly true, but as soon I saw the white envelope addressed in Nancy's handwriting sitting on Shelley's desk, I couldn't resist. I snagged it, thinking I'd just call, tell her to bring more, and pay her back when she arrived.

I brought the envelope with me that afternoon when I rode the bus out to the suburb of Kenner with Tony, who had to clean the apartment he had just moved out of near the ice rink. Back at the house there were plans for Cajun dancing, bayou tours, and a parade, but this sounded like more fun to me. We rode the streetcar downtown to Lee Circle, transferred to a city bus, then to a suburban line. As we left New Orleans proper, the Spanish oaks and older houses and pervasive air of run-down Victorian elegance gave way to a nearly generic highway, where a few po'-boy shops and drive-through daiquiri shacks bravely stood their ground between strip malls and fast-food chains.

So, I said, sitting beside him on the molded plastic bus seat, our upper arms touching, do you do heroin?

I never have, he said. I don't know why. I've done everything else.

I have some, I told him. Want to try it?

Sure.

The only problem is, I don't have any needles. Where do you get them around here?

Any grocery store. We can just stop at the Schwegmann's by the apartment complex and get some, he said.

Wow, I said, that's easy.

In New York, you had to get your sets, as we called syringes, on the street, sometimes from the same guy you bought the dope from, or more often, because there was a high degree of specialization on the Lower East Side streets where we copped, from a special needle vendor. If you wanted a little coke to go with it, you had to make a third stop. It was a hassle. If your needle got clogged or dull, you would use someone else's rather than schlep all the way across town for a new one. At the time, sharing needles was not considered a form of Russian roulette.

After the grocery store, we hiked through a series of parking lots to the apartment. Tony apologized profusely for not having any furniture, for the place being such a wreck, for not having anything to offer me to drink.

Don't worry about it, I said. You don't even live here anymore.

I sat down on a bare mattress on the floor and laid out the necessary implements: the screw-top of a soda bottle, a book of matches, the glassine packets, the syringes.

I'm going to need a glass of water and a belt, I said.

I hope I can still find a glass, Tony said, rummaging in the cabinets of the kitchenette. Okay, one glass of water and—he began to unbuckle his belt and slide it out of its loops, a gesture I found mesmerizing—one belt.

Three for two? I asked him.

What?

Oh, we usually mix three bags together, then split it two ways.

Fine, he said.

He stretched out beside me on the bed and watched me tap the packages into the bottle cap. I drew ninety milliliters of water into the syringe, shot it in into the powder, and heated the mixture over a match until it dissolved. I pulled a piece of cottony fiber out of the filter of a cigarette, rolled it into a tight ball between my thumb and forefinger, and dropped it in. Pressing the tip of the needle into the filter, I measured half the solution into first one, then the other, syringe. I turned each upside down, pulled back the plunger, and snapped my fingernail against the barrel to get the air bubbles to rise. I gently pushed the plunger back in to squeeze them out, stopping as the first drop of liquid appeared at the aperture.

Can you do yourself or do you want me to do you? I asked him.

I think I can do myself, he said.

Actually, I wasn't very adept at injections; at home, I usually had Nancy administer them for me. I had what we called "bad veins," hardly visible as tracings of blue-gray on the flesh, and always rolling away from the point of the needle. But I felt too shy to ask Tony to give me my shot at this point.

I wrapped the belt around my left arm, slipping the tongue through the buckle and pulling it tight. I flexed my arm and curled my fingers into a fist, pumping it to coax the veins out of hiding. Holding the belt taut with my teeth, I carefully inserted the needle and pulled the plunger back slightly to check that it was in the right place. Furls of ruby blood rushed into the clear liquid, indicating I had gotten it. Letting the belt slip, I injected a little of the drug, then pulled back again, mixing more blood with the liquid that remained, then put some more in, then pulled back again and waited a couple of seconds. This was the way to get the best rush, this slow process, this gradual mixing of blood and drug. I loved this part, even though it was tricky to make sure you didn't slip out of the vein midway and get a big black-and-blue mark.

As I finally pressed the plunger to the bottom, a loosening was going all through my shoulders, my intestines, inside my brain. A slight queasiness, a metallic taste in my mouth, then a kind of thudding bliss that I knew would rise and be strong and lift me up, until sadly, in a few hours, it would begin to melt away and we would have to do more. Only soon there wasn't going to be any more. I have to call Nancy, I thought with the needle barely out of my arm, and tell her to bring more. Some coke, too.

I gave Tony the belt and watched him copy my procedure, biting his lower lip in concentration. He had good veins, like Steve, the kind that bulged up from the skin and stayed put when poked.

The rest of the afternoon, I did what I could to help him as he sorted through drawers and cupboards, swept, vacuumed, dusted, and polished. He was a skilled and meticulous house-cleaner, just like my sister. A halfhearted, rag-swiping, two-hours-to-clean-one-toilet sort myself, I lived in awe of this. I toted the Formula 409 and the Ajax and the paper towels from room to room behind him, high and brave and coaxing him to tell me story after story, wanting to know everything about him, wanting the intimacy of this odd afternoon to last forever.

Tony had met Shelley in Lake Placid, New York, years ago, at the Holiday Inn coffee shop, where they both worked. He was seventeen, living in a rooming house full of skaters and training full-time for competition. She, a sophisticated older woman of twenty-two, was in art school there, as was Sandye. Pete showed up in Lake Placid around this time as well—the story was that he'd been in love with Shelley for years and she couldn't make up her mind whether he was totally wacko or just right. One day he hitchhiked in from Buffalo and showed up on her doorstep with his electric guitar and a case of beer, and that was that. He never left.

They were all close friends by the time Tony left for Europe to skate with the touring company of Holiday on Ice. After two years in the show, he returned to Philadelphia, where he lived with his parents and worked downtown, making sandwiches behind the counter of a delicatessen. The Nelly Deli, as it was known, paid barely enough to cover train fare from the suburbs, but was a good place to meet people. After a full day wrapping take-out orders and scooping coleslaw, Tony would untie his apron and hit the bars. Hey, aren't you the kid from the deli? someone would say. Let me buy you a drink.

One spring morning after the coffee-and-roll rush, Tony was lounging on a chair outside the door of the deli, smoking cigarettes and drinking a coffee himself. A small, muscular guy in tight white jeans sauntered past him into the store. Tony waited. The would-be customer poked his head back out.

You work here?

Sometimes.

You make a decent egg sandwich?

Sometimes.

You comin' in or what?

You in a hurry or what? said Tony, dropping the half-smoked cigarette and getting to his feet.

Juan waited in the doorway a beat too long for Tony to pass him smoothly. Their eyes met, almost the identical shade of brown.

Tony made the sandwich according to Juan's exacting specifications: over hard, toasted kaiser, lots of mayo, six drops Tabasco, one leaf lettuce, two slices tomato.

Should I wrap it to go?

Nah, said Juan, staring at him, I'll eat it here.

Tony was twenty and in love. He moved out of his mother's house and into Juan's apartment, cleaned for him, cooked for him, left him love notes taped inside the medicine cabinet, brought armfuls of cut flowers on the way home from work. They went to clubs almost every night, wired on pills and pot and coke and vodka and poppers or whatever else was around, Tony on the dance floor for hours while Juan sat at the bar watching everybody watch him. Eventually, he suggested that they bring one of these spectators home for the night. Tony didn't love the idea.

I want to watch him fuck you, said Juan.

Tony looked down into his drink.

Come on, coaxed Juan, but with an edge behind it.

In the morning, Tony cooked the three of them breakfast. Juan walked up behind him to look in the frying pan. Fried eggs, great, he said. We got any bread? Hey. What the fuck are you crying about now?

Other nights, if Tony protested too much, Juan and the trick would just leave the bar without him.

One unbelievably hot Fourth of July weekend, they were getting ready to go to Atlantic City. Tony was lying on the bed in his underwear, right next to the window unit, tears running down his face. He didn't make a sound, didn't want to get Juan angry.

Let's leave Philly, Tony said, making his voice sound normal.

What? said Juan. He was in the bathroom, shaving. He turned off the water.

Let's get out of the city.

What are you talking about? We're leaving in half an hour.

No, I mean, let's live someplace else.

Like where? asked Juan, running his hand along his jawline to test for smoothness.

Texas? Tony suggested. I have a friend who teaches at a rink in Austin.

Juan came out of the bathroom. Texas? he said skeptically, and then looked more closely at Tony. Oh, for God's sake, don't freak out on me. Okay, okay, Texas. Why not, let's go be cowboys.

But their stay in Austin was short-lived; it was hot as hell, their apartment sucked, Juan couldn't find a job or even a decent bar. Just as things were about to fall apart altogether, Tony received a phone call from a skating rink in New Orleans where he'd sent a résumé. They had a position for him. Juan rented a U-Haul the next day.

In New Orleans, life was once again a party. A twenty-four-hour party with cheap drinks and cheap drugs and a million guys, locals and tourists and young ones and old ones and cute ones and rich ones, leather and chains and bandannas and earrings and private clubs and back rooms. Tony was teaching little girls to do laybacks and axels and walleys at an ice rink in the suburbs. Juan had a job downtown, managing a restaurant.

And we moved into this very palace you see before you, Tony told me, turning from the windowsill he was scrubbing to gesture around the empty room with its yellowed walls and olive carpeting. Can you believe I lived here for four years?

Because it was convenient to the rink but not to Juan's work, it was perfectly reasonable that many nights Juan didn't make it home. Especially because when he did, there was always a fight. Broken plates, tears, big stupid scenes. Tony told himself at first Juan would tire of the pace and settle down; instead, he tired of Tony.

Sometimes Tony would go downtown at night, look for Juan in the bars, end up with someone else. Or he would stay home, chain-smoke, order a pizza. He had an affair with the pizza delivery man for a while. He was taking Valium, lots of Valium. The little girls at the ice rink didn't notice.

One night, he was driving home from work on Veterans Highway, and there was a cop in the street directing traffic around some construction. Tony didn't see the officer motion him to stop, so cruised right past him. A block later he was surrounded by police cars, then taken in and charged, as he told it, with everything from expired registration to DWI to assaulting a peace officer. He finally got out of the police station at 2 A.M. with a pile of tickets and a court date.

When he got home, Juan was there for once, right there in the living room with some guy Claude from the bars and old Claude was on his knees sucking Juan's dick. Tony lost it completely, slammed Claude into the wall. Then Juan punched him, and by the time it was over, Claude had to take them both to the emergency room.

After Juan moved out, Tony sat in the apartment for weeks and weeks, sleeping eighteen hours a day, watching soap operas and late-night television in between, leaving the house only in the dark before dawn to go to the rink and teach, but sometimes not even accomplishing that. Shortly before Shelley and Pete had moved to town, he had taken a bottle of downs, attempting suicide. Soon after that, he was asked to resign from the ice-rink staff; what the little girls didn't notice about his condition, their parents finally did. Then he could no longer afford the apartment and moved in briefly with Larone in the Quarter until he got tossed out of there and ended up at Shelley and Pete's place uptown.

He stopped talking abruptly, the story hanging awkwardly in the air.

This disinfectant is getting to me, said Tony. Let's open some windows.

Right before we left, Tony showed me two plastic vials he'd found in the back of a drawer.

A nurse named Kelly was staying with us for a while, he explained, and she brought this stuff home from the hospital. What's it called? Oh yeah, anapsin. One night she and I really wanted to go out, but Juan didn't want to go and he wouldn't give us the keys to the car. So she offered him a shot of the anapsin, winking at me behind his back because it was going to mellow him out totally. Juan, Mr. I'll Do Anything, snapped it right up. But right after he did it, he had like every adverse reaction in the *PDR*.

Tony suddenly stopped speaking, clapped his hand to his brow, and pulled a thick red clothbound copy of the *Physician's Desk Reference* from the drawer of an old-fashioned telephone table. He threw the book into a cardboard box of things he planned to take with him.

God, I almost left this here, he said. That would have been a crisis. Anyway, he continued, Juan was lying on the couch with his tongue hanging out, saying he was afraid he was going to swallow it. Kelly, I said, I just wanted to put him to sleep, I didn't want to kill him! She had no idea what to do.

What *did* you do? I said.

Well, I remembered from my Judy Garland book that when she OD'd they fed her like a ton of Chinese food. If it worked for Judy, I thought, it'll work for Juan. So we called out for Chinese.

What happened?

Three egg rolls and an order of General Tso's Chicken and he was good as new.

You're kidding, I said. Should we try some?

If you want to, he said.

Here's how we were then: we did it. We opened a vial of anapsin and injected it in each other's butts, like it said to on the label. Just a little, to see how it was.

It wasn't great. We didn't swallow our tongues or anything, but the rest of that day was like swimming through Vaseline. Hurrying down Canal Street to catch the streetcar in the February dusk, carrying a box of Tony's things, I tripped and fell and tore a big bloody hole in the knee of my pants.

Oh, no! Tony cried, leaving the papers to blow away as he bent down to look at my wound. Are you all right?

I'm fine, I said, my face hot with embarrassment and love and pharmaceuticals. It's nothing. I do this all the time.

IRIS AND BACCHUS

We had been in New Orleans for five days when I finally made it to a parade, though it was just a few blocks from Pete and Shelley's to the route on St. Charles. The gates of the mansions were flung open and their balconies filled with people, as were the sidewalks and streetcar track before them. The grand boulevard had abandoned itself to the spirit of the celebration, with purple bikini underwear and helium balloons looped over the wrought-iron fences, concession trucks on every corner, and bleachers set up on the lawns.

Only the weather refused to cooperate, relentlessly cold and gray as it had been all week. As the last day before Lent, Mardi Gras is tied to the lunar calendar and moves around each year between February and March. When it falls at the early end of the range, as it had that year, the weather can be seriously unconducive to outdoor festivities. But the New Orleanians don't let a little thing like pneumonia get in their way.

I kept my eyes on the thin white line parting Shelley's carroty pigtails so I wouldn't lose her as we threaded through the throng, the parked cars, the coolers and stepladders spilling into each intersection. Behind me were Sandye and the rest of the out-of-towners; Tony and Pete were bringing up the rear, dragging the beer in a wagon. It was a morning when beer for breakfast was de rigueur, the Saturday before Fat Tuesday, province of the all-woman Krewe of Iris.

Shelley stopped at the first clear patch of sidewalk, in front of a florist's window filled with irises and daffodils. She began shov-

ing beers into rubber cool-cans and handing them around, giving instructions on where to meet if someone got lost.

As far uptown as we were, as early as it was in the morning,
local residents far outnumbered the tourists. But even the most
venerable citizens dressed for the parades in souvenir-shop re-
galia: green-, yellow-, and purple-striped polo shirts, cutoff
midriff tops, pompom antennae caught at a former year's parade. Children were everywhere: lining the curbs, clustered
around soda vendors, piled on the hoods of cars, stuffed into
plywood loge boxes nailed to stepladders, from where they ran-
domly spilled their Cokes on people's heads.

The first vehicles to come down the boulevard were converted grocery carts pushed by itinerant vendors. Multicolored
Afro wigs, cotton candy, and bags of fluorescent popcorn swung
from metal racks as they raced along. Following them, a New
Orleans Public Service truck with a measuring pole went by to
make sure the tallest floats wouldn't hit the electric lines, its appearance drawing the crowd to the curbs in anticipation.

Moments later a police van rolled past, followed by the
omnipresent Shriners. Dignitaries in polished convertibles
tossed the first doubloons—large plastic coins stamped with the
year and the krewe's insignia. High school bands played Mardi
Gras standards, regal young women in sequined maillots and
sparkling white boots marched to disco songs booming from
sound trucks. Painted barques full of goddesses rolled behind
them, Olympian riders reaching between immense papier-
mâché flowers to shower necklaces and plastic cups and rayon
undergarments on the crowd. The frenzy to catch these was intense, driving even adults to bratty child behavior, snatching
beads out of the air inches away from a small open hand.

I ran into the K&B drugstore for a carton of Merits and a
bottle of vodka. On the way out, I passed a display of Valentine's

Day cards and candy, and added a heart-shaped box of chocolates to my purchases. As I pushed through the exit door, I pulled my sweater around me and sashayed across the street to the beat of a zydeco band. Tony was surrounded by little kids to whom he was passing out the necklaces he'd just caught, a whole sheaf of pink ones still bound together with a loop from the factory. I found a cup on the ground, filled it with vodka and gave it to him, flashing a coquettish smile. But when I went to pull the red foil box of candy out of the bag, I hesitated a moment, suddenly shy, confused about where the parody ended and real life began.

I know Valentine's Day isn't till Monday, but—

You silly girl, he said, smiling at me, setting the drink down so he could open the box. Vodka and chocolate, breakfast of champions. But I don't have anything for you.

Oh, I replied huskily, back on track again, I wouldn't say that.

If this was a game, it was becoming a rather consuming one. For almost a week, I'd spent every possible minute in his presence, paying not much attention to Shelley, Pete, Sandye, or the rest of the gang, becoming a semipermanent fixture on the corner stool at the bar where he worked double shifts. Since Nancy had arrived with the reinforcements, I had drugs again; we'd slip into the bathroom every few hours and get high. The other bartenders and waiters at the Fatted Calf liked me a lot. They laughed at my jokes and called me Diana Rigg because of the needles, the "rigs," I carried in my pocket. When they got really busy, I would help bus tables and take names for the waiting list. I told everyone I was going to get a sex change so I could be Tony's boyfriend.

The Calf was ordinarily a quiet watering hole and hamburger joint favored by gay residents of the Quarter. It was a long, narrow place with a shotgun layout: bar and jukebox in front, tables and chairs in the middle, kitchen in the rear. With its teak-stained wooden floors, walls, and furnishings, it was dark and cool as a cellar at all times of day. But due to its central location on St. Peter Street, the placid Calf was transformed during Mardi Gras to a raging Bull, a raucous madhouse full of carnival customers. This group was unified not by any particular sexual orientation but by its single-minded intention to get drunk as fast and party as long as possible. Drinks were served not only to the tables and over the bar, but out the window to those passing on the sidewalk and through the upper half of a Dutch door to another crowd in the alley.

Over this throng, Tony presided in a black vest and white shirt with the sleeves rolled up, always smiling. In one velvety motion, he would slide from one end of the bar to the other to deliver a clutch of cocktails, then twirl back to stuff a fistful of cash in the register. Even if you didn't know he was a skater, you couldn't help but notice his gracefulness; as it was, I kept imagining that fluidity, that quick, balletic precision on ice. As the night wore on and the floor got slipperier, his spins and stops and glides became so flamboyant that other customers caught on. Skate over this way, baby, someone shouted from the end of the bar, and bring me a beer. All right! Beautiful! That's a 5.9 for artistic expression from the East German judge!

Occasionally, Marcellina, the skinny black woman who cooked the burgers, would come out for a break and sit beside me at the bar. She told me stories like the one about how her husband stole her TV set and took it over to his girlfriend's place, and when she got home from work and the neighbors told her what had happened, she ran over to the other woman's apartment and found them in bed watching Carson on her goddamn TV. So naturally she shot him in the dick.

Did it kill him? I asked.

I wish, said Marcellina, sucking on her long, skinny menthol cigarette. Hey, Tony, gimme another Courvoisier, Coke back.

Finally, we would get out of there at three or so and walk over to the Bourbon Pub. There were better bars, Tony said, but they didn't allow women in.

Despite their flexible rules, the Pub was jammed only with men; the sole exceptions were me and Madonna, who throbbed out of the speakers and pouted down from the video screens. The dance floor was upstairs, a room so liquid black that when you first entered you didn't know if you were in a closet or an auditorium. Then ribbons of pink and green and blue and yellow light shot from the ceiling in every direction, reflected a zillion times in the mirrored walls, bounced through the glass doors onto the balcony, and landed on the faces and arms of the dancers.

Dancing with Tony was the penultimate nail in the coffin of my self-control. I could see how it must have been in those bars in Philadelphia with Juan; when Tony cut loose on the dance floor, people couldn't help watch. Those long limbs and tight muscles, those full lips and half-closed eyes, that perfect rhythm—he was so sexy, it wasn't even fair. Mesmerized by his graceful, jazzy, understated moves, I wasn't dancing the way I normally do at all, but almost unconsciously copying his gestures, reflecting him as if we were making love. Which was exactly what I had in mind. It was going to take a little doing, that was certain, but I was too caught up in my own desire to think it impossible.

I was also too caught up in my desire to avoid the fight with Nancy that had threatened all week. Like me, she had had reservations about Mardi Gras in the first place, then I had stolen her dope and Sandye was dragging half of New York City along. But Steve, Nancy's boyfriend of six years, was planning on going down, and it would be her only chance to see him for a while.

He'd been out in Vegas visiting his parents, and after New Orleans, he was off on another trip. So she had to go. Not that they
would have two minutes alone together, as she told me irritably.

To top it off, she had come down with laryngitis the minute
she stepped off the plane into the New Orleans terminal and
then arrived at Shelley and Pete's to find a noisy mob scene:
drunkards, giggling maniacs, people doing Royal Canadian
Mountie calisthenics, and most ridiculous of all, me, her idiotic
older sister, making an utter spectacle of myself over Tony, the
gay ice-skater.

He was nice, yes, funny, yes, good-looking, yes, but homo-
sexual, yes, yes, yes. It wasn't a secret, everyone knew it, it was
as if "the gay ice-skater" were part of his name. And there I was,
wearing his clothes already, a black tux jacket and a T-shirt that
said LOUISIANA—A DREAM STATE. Indeed. I was following him
around and virtually ignoring everyone else. It was crystal-clear
to her that it was in an attempt to impress this new love of my
life that I had hijacked her drugs.

In fact, her reaction was not unreasonable. For the past thirteen months, since Jordan, the last love of my life, had abandoned me, I had been wallowing in the worst case of obsessive
despair imaginable, as if all the disappointments preceding it
were just summer stock and *Heartbreak with Jordan* was my
Broadway premiere. I had been drinking and smoking and
speedballing myself to death, committing an extended public
suicide for the benefit of my poor ex-boyfriend. Nancy had been
understanding for quite a while, but after many attempts to
cheer me up or at least distract me, she just could not feel sorry
for me anymore. The idea that I was going to pick myself up,
turn around, and run straight off another cliff was more than she
could stand.

In addition to the main room, Pete and Shelley's apartment

included a kitchenette, a bathroom, and a foyer with a stained-glass window just inside the front door. Sleeping arrangements were tight: Pete and Shelley were on the bed, Sandye, Tony, the other New Yorkers, and I were on the floor, and Nancy and Steve were sleeping under Shelley's printmaking table in the foyer.

I had managed to squirm my sleeping bag in next to Tony's every night so far, once actually dragging the sleeping body of my writing-program friend several feet across the floor, but the foyer was the only place that afforded enough privacy for the activities I had in mind. So I decided to switch with Nancy. She'd had her turn, right? But when she saw me shuffling the sleeping bags around, she went berserk.

What the hell are you doing with my sleeping bag, she croaked in her laryngitis rasp.

Um, I was trading places with you for the night.

I don't think so, said Nancy. Give me my sleeping bag.

I just stood there, so she grabbed it. We tugged it back and forth between us.

What's the matter with you, Nancy, I hissed. What's the big deal?

You tell me, she said. You tell me what the fucking big deal is.

She let go of the sleeping bag and I hit the floor. Forget it, I said, my butt smarting from the fall. You're such a bitch.

I went and locked myself in the bathroom, my plans foiled.

That night was Bacchus, a parade known as the largest and most extravagant of Carnival. William Shatner rode in the first car as its king, followed by floats that were whole blocks long: King Kong, Mrs. Kong, and Baby Kong, the famous Bacchagator, a new-for-this-year procession of gargantuan pinup girls, led by Marilyn Monroe. Bent over to blow a pouty red kiss, her thighs were eye level to people standing on a third-story balcony, her cleavage tantalizing those on the fourth. The beads they tossed from the floats were ugly, though—fat purple plastic grapes hung with cheap gold-lettered medallions.

I let Tony go to work by himself that night and went along with the gang to the parade, but Nancy was not appeased. We were completely out of dope by then, which didn't help her mood either. I could see it would not be worth trying to reopen the subject of the foyer.

Still, that night after everyone was asleep, I lay on Shelley and Pete's floor beside Tony, studying his profile in the shadowy moonlight. Very gently, I slid closer and laid my head on his chest. His heartbeat was surprisingly strong for that slim body, slow and regular and loud.

I had almost fallen asleep to its rhythm when he shifted so my head slipped into the crook of his arm, then leaned over and put his lips on mine. They hovered there for a moment, then opened slightly. I felt his breath, his heat, the chip in his tooth, the tip of his tongue. I lay absolutely still, as if he were a wild animal I didn't want to alarm. He moved his fingers along my neck, and my whole body shivered with longing.

Then he kissed me again, a brush of lips on my cheek accompanied by a squeeze of unmistakable finality, rolled over, and went to sleep.

Practically on fire, I curled myself around him spoonwise and stared into the dark.

I can't believe I have to go home, I said, twirling my spoon in my coffee. The Denny's was quiet; Mardi Gras was in its final hours. It was almost Wednesday morning.

Me either, he said. I don't want you to go.

My heart was in my throat. I wanted to say I love you, I can't leave you, please make love to me right this minute.

What do you think is going on with us? I finally tried.

I don't know, he said, and took a drag off his cigarette. It's pretty intense.

Yeah, I agreed. Intense.

We both pushed our food around our plates for a while.

Can't you come back? he asked.

Definitely. I'm coming back this summer, I said, making it up as I went along. I'll come down and spend the summer after I finish my M.F.A., before I go to law school or whatever.

Law school?

Oh, I applied to law school for the fall, I explained. I thought it might do me some good. Straighten me out.

In my head, going to law school was the equivalent of committing myself to a mental institution or joining the army, a sensible alternative to staying in New York and killing myself. I needed a change of scenery and a printed schedule. If I had to study law to get it, that was okay by me.

Well, by this summer I should have an apartment, Tony said. In the Quarter. You can stay with me. It'll be a blast.

I smiled at him. Yeah, I said. It will.

A few hours later, I piled into the steamy hangovermobile with the rest of them, tears pouring down my face, twisting around to get the last possible glimpse of Tony before we turned the corner on Prytania. Lines from love poems by Frank O'Hara and Allen Ginsberg were in my head, and that's who I wanted to be—that passionate outlaw poet with his beautiful taboo love.

SWIMMING WITH SHARKS

The next few weeks of my life were devoted to subsidizing my long-distance carrier, as Tony and I spent the majority of our waking hours on the phone. He would call me from everywhere—Pete and Shelley's, the store on the corner, the phone at work—or, after he got off, from the Pub, 2 A.M. gay-bar collect calls that went on for hours, so much background noise we could hardly hear each other. I'd be in the freezing kitchen of our apartment on Sixteenth Street, wrapped in a blanket, shouting into the phone until somebody stumbled out to tell me to keep it down. Then a song like "I'm So Excited" by the Pointer Sisters or "Genius of Love" by the Tom Tom Club would come on and he'd say, Oh God, listen to this, and put down the phone and dance while I actually listened.

I heard from Shelley that he had a photo of me taken during Mardi Gras that he carried around with him everywhere. I was on Bourbon Street on Fat Tuesday, a dozen ropes of colored beads around my neck, posing with two older women dressed up as seafood platters. They wore tablecloths festooned with clamshells and crawfish heads and packets of Wash 'n Dri; red lobster claws poked crazily from their straw hats.

Whenever we go out to eat, Shelley told me, he takes out the picture and sets it up against the napkin-holder. Sometimes he orders you a cup of coffee.

This was a sign, one I recognized immediately. For the first time in my life, I had gotten fixated on someone who could fixate back.

I got busy explaining to everyone I knew in New York how I'd met this incredible gay ice-skater in New Orleans, love at first sight, the real actual thing. I paid no attention to their responses, which were not enthusiastic. They had it on authority as high as Dear Abby that things like this never worked out. Sandye thought I was nuts, and Nancy was barely speaking to me since our fight at Mardi Gras. Only Pete, down in New Orleans, was enthusiastic. He said he knew this was going to happen, had been waiting to fix us up for years. This sounded like a joke, but with Pete, you could never tell.

Of all the people I regaled with my exciting new romance, I most enjoyed telling my ex-boyfriend Jordan, who had caused me to throw the entire preceding year of my life into the dark waste-basket of unrequited love. *I am free of your spell, ha-ha-ha* was my message for him. In fact, he was probably more relieved than I.

Unlike my interest in Tony, which appeared in my life as suddenly and dwarfed everything else as completely as a skyscraper built next door to one's house in the night, my interest in Jordan had developed gradually. He was my coworker in the research department at Stanley H. Kaplan Educational Center, or SHKEC, which we pronounced like some Yiddish term of derision, a place where they hired kids out of college with high test scores to write courses to help other people improve theirs. At first, Jordan was just part of the scenery at SHKEC, okay-looking, tall, skinny, degree from Brandeis in Jewish studies. My favorite thing about him was his silly imitation of Big Bird.

Isn't it strange how you can know somebody for months or even years and it's nothing dramatic, then you realize one morning you've gone and fallen in love? Like in a handheld home video, where some tiny figure way across the lawn on a blanket is suddenly in close-up and you see the color of his eyes, how the muscles move in his face.

My awareness of Jordan peaked during a big deadline crisis at work, when the two of us were assigned to develop a set of reading-comprehension exercises together. In the ten days we spent madly typing sheets of questions and answers on our IBM Selectrics and trading them over the Plexiglas wall that separated our carrels, he became my soulmate. *Which of the following best characterizes the relationship between William Wordsworth and his sister Dorothy? How does the author feel about current trends in biomedical research? If all Swedes are thrifty, do some of the fishermen in Malmö wear plaid flannel workshirts? Pusillanimous is to Pugnacity as Mendacious is to . . . Oleaginousness? Valor? Probity? Lasciviousness?*

He was brilliant, he was funny, he was a writer. He was Jewish, he spoke French, he was in therapy. He didn't do drugs, which could be a good thing, I thought, a beneficial influence. As I borrowed and read his paperback editions of Philip Roth and Milan Kundera, falling in love with those authors was all tangled up in my mind with falling in love with him. When I look at the zillions of notes we passed back and forth at work—which I still have, along with ticket stubs from *My Dinner with André* and the little ad he ran on my birthday on the back page of *The Village Voice*—they are so filled with our lost intimacy that I can't understand them anymore, as if they were written in a foreign language about another world.

After three months, to my utter surprise, he said we had to stop seeing each other.

I was too intense, he said.

The drugs were scaring him, he said.

It wasn't just me, he said, it was my sister, our friends, our crazy apartment on Sixteenth Street—the whole package was too much.

He had his own problems, he said. He wasn't ready for this.

Nothing he said made any sense to me at all. I was as bewildered as if I had come home from school one day and found my family had moved, the house empty, a FOR SALE sign stuck in the yard. I spent the whole next year pounding on his door, alternating between despair and trying to get him back, drinking more and more vodka, shooting up three, then four, then five days a week, even at work. Especially at work, where the pain of seeing him every day was intolerable. Where he would have to notice how my eyes were red from crying, how the track marks were creeping down my arms.

At the time, I too was seeing a therapist, but how much she was able to help me was limited by our failure to agree on the nature of my problem. I always wanted to talk about Jordan. She thought the bigger issue was heroin. Why, why, why, she wanted to know.

Drugs, big deal, was my answer at the time, but in retrospect, I think we were just looking at different sides of the same self-destructive coin. I can't say I've grown out of these tendencies altogether, but I'm a paragon of self-esteem and sanity compared to who I was in my teens and twenties. Back then, I had enough ambient self-loathing to make anything possible.

I recently heard the writer Tim Cahill on the radio talking about how he went swimming with a school of sharks to forget the obsession with human evil he had developed after spending years doing research on serial killers. *To make everything else go away except my own life or death,* he said. That line gave me goose bumps of recognition. Perhaps if I had had more physical self-confidence, I would have chosen more salutary high-risk pastimes, like white-water rafting or Arctic exploration or walking across the desert barefoot. As it was, drugs and love were the only way I knew to dissolve my boundaries, to escape, to turn down the voices in my head.

God knows, I would do anything not to be boring. It was a

serious lifelong project. I mean, I was a middle-class Jewish girl from suburban New Jersey. Not much of a résumé for the fascinating, dangerous bohemian character I knew I was meant to be. I was well aware that romantic obsession and self-abuse were essential characteristics for an artist, like my tattoo, my inveterate hitchhiking, and my gray fedora. Caution and safety were hopelessly bourgeois concepts.

At the time, I saw "don't do heroin" as no different than "don't walk down Avenue C by yourself" or "don't eat abandoned french fries off someone else's table in a restaurant." The word *no* was my cue, my call to arms. The minute someone said I shouldn't do something or couldn't have something, *this is not allowed, don't go in there, stay away,* every cell in my body rushed toward it, every synapse in my brain started firing. I had to turn that *no* into a *yes* or die trying. Though most people stop before they stick a needle in their arm, it was against my personal code of honor to be afraid of anything.

And in the end, I loved the needles almost as much as the stuff inside them. I loved seeing my blood, playing with it, changing its chemistry. I loved the scariness of it, the tiny prick of pain. The absolute focus required. The way when someone else does it for you, it's almost like sex. I was the suburban boho wannabe with something extra—a death wish, a relentless loneliness that drove me always a little bit further than "a nice girl like you" might be imagined to go.

If I couldn't dissolve my boundaries emotionally, I could do it with chemicals. If I couldn't merge, I could at least black out. You say you don't want me? Fine. I can make that pain go away. Let me show you.

SLOW DANCE

When the phone bill came at the end of the month, I concluded it would be cheaper to fly back down and talk to Tony in person. Summer was too far away, we both agreed. Perhaps Tony still thought of me as his personal fag hag, platonic groupie, party sidekick, gay-man-trapped-in-a-woman's body—the roles I had cast myself in during the Mardi Gras visit. But we were about to run into a snag. No matter how fascinated I was by gayness and gay culture, I was not, in fact, ever going to be a gay man. If we were really to be in love, something else had to give.

I returned to New Orleans in March wearing a tight red-and-white zebra print wraparound dress with a deep V-neck, something I'd rescued from the closet of my Aunt Edie, who in her day had been a chorus girl in a burlesque show. When they saw me prance off the plane from New York in that dress, complete with an inch and a half of cleavage and white high heels, Pete and Shelley and Tony just laughed.

What? I demanded. You don't like my ensemble? You don't think it's me?

By this time, I was a supernova of sexual energy, ready to implode or explode or probably plode simultaneously in both directions. I could feel it like a motor, revving somewhere deep in my body all the time. But the mechanics of the situation were less than ideal. Tony had not yet moved into his French Quarter apartment, so again we stayed at Pete and Shelley's, sleeping on the floor of the famous foyer. Foyer or no, Tony was avoiding the possibility of sex. We'd stay out at the bars all night or home drinking with Pete

and Shelley until we were cross-eyed with exhaustion, then fall into
our sleeping bags. By the time I assumed my seductive position and
offered a tentative caress, he was asleep.

During the day, when he wasn't working, we got started on
the project of spending my life savings, eating out constantly and
buying whatever—Mardi Gras posters, trendy shoes, new hair-
cuts for both of us from a friend of his. It wasn't like he talked
me into this. I wanted to spend money on him. It was the best
way I had to express my feelings at the time. We went to expensive tourist bars and ordered the biggest frozen drinks on the
menu, then paid twenty bucks to have the house photographer
take our picture: me with my long-sleeved Go-Go's T-shirt, him
in a leather jacket. I still have that picture—we barely look old
enough to drink.

One night, he lay his head in my lap and let me pierce his ear.
I used ice cubes and a shot of whiskey to get him numb, then did
the job with a sterilized safety pin. I took off one of my diamond
studs and slipped it into the brand-new hole. His eyelids flut-
tered open.

That wasn't so bad, he said.

I told you I wouldn't hurt you, I answered, smoothing back a
lock of hair from his forehead.

That's what they all say, he replied.

We did finally fuck, and that's about all you could say for it. It
was the night we went to see Iggy Pop at Jimmy's, a barnlike
club with a bar and a stage and a guy the size of a small island at
the door. It was one of those nights when people you don't even
know are giving you Mandrax and shoving lines of cocaine up
your nose. You couldn't get near the front, so I stood next to a
speaker, high as a kite, croaking along with Iggy. Somehow I got
fixated on a broom, a very nice industrial-quality, black-bristled
broom, clearly equal to the task of sweeping out a seedy bar

night after night. I knew as soon as I saw it, I had to have it. Maybe I thought I needed it to sweep the debris out of my life and set up housekeeping with Tony. I grabbed it from its spot in a corner and danced it wildly around the floor as if we were a thrash rock Fred and Ginger.

When we got back to the house, broom in tow, Tony went suddenly and inexplicably nuts. I think he was jealous of the guy who had been giving me the coke, or just mad because he didn't get any, but in any case he flipped out and started yelling about how I was the Genius of Bullshit, not the Genius of Love as previously suggested, and then got into this out-of-the-blue anti-Semitic stuff about how I should go back to Israel.

Even an apparent psychotic break could not deter me from my purpose. When he finally stopped ranting and lay down, I went over and lay beside him, worried and upset but still stupid with lust. I watched his face as I ran my fingertips gently over his forearm, a gesture pitched halfway between soothing and seduction. For a moment he just kept his eyes closed, but then he reached over and pulled me to him and he wasn't kissing me as much as pressing his face into mine and before I knew it we were having sex, a quick, rough, unsexy kind of sex that scared me. Poor Shelley and Pete, in their little bed just around the corner, trying to pretend nothing was going on.

Did you ever make love to a girl before? I finally got up the nerve to ask him the next night after he got off from work. The suddenness and brusqueness of our sexual encounter had finally made me realize the magnitude of what I was asking from Tony. After all my big talk in New York, I now wondered if the obstacles to our romance were more serious than I had imagined.

Yeah, once, he said. I was about sixteen. We were in the woods. I don't remember much about it.

You didn't like it?

I definitely didn't like the woods, he said. Too much dirt and bugs and sharp little twigs.

Poor Miss Priss, I said.

Oh, shut up, he replied.

So after that you slept with guys?

No, after that I only fucked indoors. Actually, it was a little later, when I was living in Lake Placid. I met these dancers from the Paul Taylor company who were in town for the summer— that's when I figured it out.

That you were gay?

That or a very weird straight guy with a thing for male dancers.

You were, what, eighteen?

Yeah, about eighteen. So what do you want to do? You want to have a drink somewhere?

Sure, I said. Let's go see Deedee.

Tony's friend Deedee played piano in the lounge of the Andrew Jackson Hotel. A longtime denizen of the Quarter, she sang old standards in a smoky voice, decked out in feathered, sequined evening gowns and towering blond wigs with rhinestone combs. I thought at first she was a drag queen, but Tony said no, she was a real woman.

Deedee took a motherly interest in Tony and was pleased when we started coming around together. She was the only person among Tony's acquaintances who assumed instantly that we were an item.

Hello, Tony the Pony, she called in between numbers. Howdy, Miss Marion. Ah'm so glad y'all came by. You got a drink? Are you hungry? I'll have them bring you something over from the restaurant.

Deedee sent bowls of oyster-and-artichoke soup to our

table, I ordered a bottle of champagne, and between that and the sweet old songs—Deedee sang "Embraceable You," "Moon River," and always, for Tony, "Over the Rainbow"—I was suddenly, loonily, happy. We slow-danced that night for the first time. Neither of us had any idea what we were doing, and at first we were laughing and whirling around, but then he pulled me close and we barely moved, just leaned on each other with our eyes closed.

I could feel the hard muscles in his thighs, his breath in my hair, his heart beating against my cheek as I lay against him. I knew that heart to be as vulnerable and as barely glued back together as my own. I tightened my arms around him; he slid his hands gently down my back. It seemed to me in that moment that if there were obstacles to our relationship, they were no greater than those we faced apart.

I was leaving again. We kissed goodbye at the airport while Pete and Shelley stood in the background, waving and looking relieved to see me go. I was wearing the same trampy outfit I'd worn on the way down, seeing as I was not much less sexually frustrated and even more emotionally overwound.

The man in the seat beside me liked my cheesy dress a whole damn lot, I could tell. He asked if he could buy me a drink, and I ordered a double since that's what he was having. Not a bad-looking guy, he was still growing out his hair from being in the Marines; he had very black, sparkly eyes and a country-boy way of talking that was quite appealing at the time. Soon we were drunk and I was telling him my tale of woe. Why're you wastin' yourself on a guy like that, he asked me, and I just shook my head and made a who-knows face. By then, his hand had appeared on my leg, and I didn't do a thing about it.

When the stewardess came by and asked if anyone needed a

blanket, I knew it was all over. With that fuzzy blue thing covering about one square foot of our bodies, in the half-dark of the evening flight, my hand slipped inside his shirt, the wraparound dress unwrapped, he was running his tongue along my neck and shoulder as if I were a melting ice-cream cone. All of this was done in total silence. That and the fact that we stopped somewhere short of penetration were our only concessions to the fact that we were on a crowded airplane.

When the stewardess prodded me, I woke up with a start. Do you think you could put your seat belt on, please? she asked a little sarcastically. We're about to land.

I untangled myself and tried to fix my dress and find my seat belt. What's-his-name woke up too and we were embarrassed, but not as embarrassed as you might think. We didn't trade phone numbers or addresses.

Everything that happened to me those first months of knowing Tony I wrote down in a datebook. I had always used a datebook to keep track of my plans, but during that time I was more thorough than usual. Every block of the calendar was scribbled with names of restaurants and bars and bands, phrases like "Terrible Fight!" and "Full Moon," penciled tallies of the amount of money spent on drugs and, eventually but not frequently, a special symbol to indicate that we'd had sex.

I lost the datebook later that summer when we left New Orleans for good, and I mourned it like I should have been mourning all the brain cells I was killing every day with my reckless lifestyle. I wanted to remember it all so much, every minute of it, and now when I look back, it is mostly just a blur of barbecued shrimp and disco music and desire.

I could feel my life changing around me, momentum building beneath me as if I were bodysurfing. Part of the current was holding my feet to the ground, even pulling me back, but if I could spring at the right moment to catch the forward thrust, the wave would take me all the way to shore. I had to pay very close attention so I would know when it was time.

When I got home from that second visit and announced my plan to quit my job at SHKEC, finish my master's degree by mail, and move to New Orleans, all my friends said I was just running away from my problems. They were right, I was, but I thought it worth a try.

Only Aunt Edie of the zebra dress gave me her blessing, though admittedly I'd told her an edited version of the story. To her, Tony sounded like a fine young man and New Orleans was a thrilling place. Edie was from the *South Pacific* school of romance management. You know what they say, Marion, she told me. Once you have found him, never let him go.

BACK EAST

Tony arrived on the doorstep of the apartment I shared with Nancy and Steve and Sandye on a fine evening in early April. Though his appearance was no surprise—I'd bought the plane ticket—I remember opening that door and being knocked over by the fact that he was there, beautiful as ever, in a leather jacket, blue jeans, suede boots, and his perennial Ray-Ban Baloramas.

Hey, Tony, I said.

Hey, Mar, he said, dropping his bag and stepping over the threshold. We kissed for a nervous minute, then just when I couldn't stand it anymore, he pulled away and said, Got anything to drink? I'm dying of thirst.

Tony was in town to help me pack and drive my car back to New Orleans to live with him. We planned to stay in the area for three weeks or so before heading down. I had tickets to a play, dates for him to meet my friends and family, big ideas about museums, matinees, restaurants, galleries. Of course in the end we lay around the apartment half of every day and spent the rest of the time wandering aimlessly around the Village, returning to the apartment after Steve and Nancy got home from their construction and bookkeeping jobs for an L.E.S. Club meeting, as my roommates and I called our nightly drugfests.

Steve was president of the Lower East Side Club, named for the neighborhood where we purchased our supplies. Nancy was the treasurer, a rather important function, and I was the secretary. Sandye thought the whole thing was ridiculous, though every once in a while she'd have Steve get her a dime bag, then stick it in her jewelry box and nip at it for months.

You can be the member, Steve told Tony at his first official meeting. We need a member.

Later that night, he took Tony out on one of his graffiti expeditions. Steve had gone to art school in Kansas City and New York, and still painted on the side. His contribution to the graffiti art explosion in New York in the early eighties was a series of wall paintings made by dipping a T-shirt into paint, printing its image on the wall, then decorating it with spray-painted dots or lines. His tag was Fall Fashions. Ultimately, a museum in Texas commissioned Fall Fashions to decorate a wall of a boarded-up building downtown and his outlaw status was compromised, but it was worth it, I thought, to see those rows and rows of drippy, lighthearted pastel silhouettes right on the corner of Sixth and Congress.

When Steve and Tony came back from their outing that night, they were deep in a conversation about Grandmaster Flash and Jean-Michel Basquiat; male bonding was under way. The two of them had gotten along well enough at Mardi Gras, but during this visit, they fell in love with each other in the way people who are going to be very good friends do. Though one was a gay ice-skater and the other a somewhat macho construction worker, they were the same age and from similar working-class Italian backgrounds; they shared passions for travel, avant-garde art, gardening, black music, and drugs. This last was a form of recreation that gave them something to do together, as if they both liked to play handball or rebuild engines. They would get high and make cassette tape compilations of songs they liked, flipping through old copies of *Architectural Digest* between record changes.

We had this silly thing where we called each other nicknames based on taking the first letters of our names and combining them with the suffix "ali." I was Mali Wali, Nancy was Nali Wali, Steve was Stali Cali. The Ali theme song was sung to the tune of "Wooly Bully," and had a variety of lyrics which began with a phrase like "Mali told Nali . . ." and went on to dramatize our drug-related exploits. During this visit, Tony became Tali Hali, and I knew he was part of the family. Later, I modified this to Beau Tali, with Boner and even Bone-Puss as variants. Tony almost always called me Mali Wali, Mali, or just Mal. These nicknames seemed to certify our status as lovers, fulfilling my wistful wonderings in the Canal Villere.

So what is the story with you two? Nancy asked me one night as I was half-helping her do the dishes. I thought he was supposed to be gay.

Oh, I don't know, Nancy. It doesn't really seem to matter.

Well, you sleep together, right?

Yes.

Do you have sex?

It's not really about sex, I told her. It's about being together.

Let's see how long you sing that tune, my sister said.

You just don't understand how it is, Nancy. I just have this feeling about us. I feel great with him.

Well, I hope it works out, Nancy said. I'd hate to see you get hurt again.

Why does everybody keep going on about me getting hurt? Why can't anyone just be happy for me?

Calm down, Marion. We're happy for you. As long as you're happy, we're happy for you.

With my mother and father, with whom we went down to have dinner at their golf club in New Jersey, things went less smoothly. Tony was not what they had in mind for me. Jordan, my Brandeis Jewish studies major, would have been perfect. Too bad he blew me off. However, since I had been turning up with more or less unsuitable boyfriends for years, my parents were used to it. At least Tony was well groomed, which counted for a lot with my mother. She greeted him warmly—Marion's told us so much about you!—and my dad made a round of cocktails. Then we went to get dressed for dinner.

What a terrific suit, my mother commented as we were leaving the house. Tony was wearing the suit I'd just bought him in New York. Well, he needed one. I didn't think twice about it. I would have spent every cent I had on him and then gone out to make more.

Yeah, isn't it great, said Tony, we just got it today at Barney's. It's a Kenzo, on sale from twelve hundred dollars down to six hundred.

My mother shot me a look but didn't say anything more on the subject until the next morning.

You bought him that suit, didn't you, she said. We were the only ones up yet, alone in the kitchen.

No big deal, I said.

Are you out of your mind? she wondered. Since when is a six-hundred-dollar suit no big deal? Are you sick? Don't you get it? This guy is a goddamn gigolo!

The conversation went straight downhill from there. It concluded with my informing her that if she wanted to be a part of my life in the future, she would have to rethink her position about Tony. If I had to choose between her and him, I would choose him, I said, and alluded ominously to grandchildren she would never see.

Oh, now you're going to marry him and have his children? she inquired incredulously. I don't know what kind of dreamworld you live in, Marion.

Despite the dramatic tenor of our pronouncements, the disagreement was more or less forgotten by lunchtime. Never having agreed on much of anything, my mother and I were expert at leaving a quarrel behind and moving onto the next order of business, which was often eating or drinking. We could always get back to the argument another time.

Thus, over a decade later, my mother was still making comments about that suit.

The whole time we were up north, I kept wondering if Tony didn't want to go see his family in Pennsylvania, but he didn't.

Why don't you ever call your mother? I asked him as we headed south on I-95, my blue Honda Civic packed with my belongings, two days and nights on the road ahead of us. I knew he was close to her, but I had yet to see him talk to her on the phone.

I'll call her soon.

But we were so nearby. Don't you think she's worried about you?

Could you shut up?

What about your father?

Fuck my father, he said. I don't even know his phone number.

Tony's parents, Grace Ann Ciocca and Edwin Heubach, were just seventeen and eighteen respectively when he was born on a military base in Illinois. By the time he was six, they were divorced; he told me he'd had to testify in the judge's chambers about his father's violence. Did he hit you? I asked, shocked. Abusive fathers were something I had only read about in books.

Yeah. Though mostly he went after my mother. Especially if he came home drunk from a hard day balling his girlfriend in the back of his cop car and she didn't have the floors waxed or something.

He's a policeman?

Yeah, a fucking narcotics detective, if you can believe it. The only good thing he ever did for me was get my speeding tickets fixed. The last time I talked to him was five years ago, right after I got home from Europe.

Tony and Juan had gone to see *Madame Butterfly* with a wealthy older friend of theirs, a big opera queen. After the show, they stopped at an Irish bar that had, their friend said, the best corned-beef sandwiches in town. They were at a table in the back drinking their beers and eating their sandwiches when Tony realized that the red-faced, jowly loudmouth at the bar, the one he'd been glaring at for the past ten minutes, was his father. He hadn't seen him in years. After the divorce, Eddie used to come pick up Tony and his brother Frankie every summer and take them to their grandmother's fishing camp out in the woods. After a few times, Tony would disappear as soon as he saw Eddie's car in the driveway.

He would have disappeared this time too. Would have sneaked out of the bar when his father's back was turned, would have pretended it never happened. Only Eddie saw him first.

He lumbered over to the table; they exchanged a few pleasantries. How's your mother? You need money? Lemme buy you a beer. Then Eddie allowed as to how he had heard Tony was a fag, and it was disgusting, it made him sick.

I thought he was going to hit me, Tony said, or spit on the table or something, but he just stood there for a second, boiling, then turned and walked out.

Tony preferred to tell stories about his grandfather, Valdrick, a gentle Old World character who grew figs and tomatoes and basil, who fished every day, who hunted squirrels and rabbits in the woods behind the house in the Poconos and made spaghetti sauce out of them. During the chaotic period at the end of her marriage to Eddie, Grace had left Tony and Frankie in the care of her parents, and Valdrick had become a hero and a role model to Tony in the way his own father never would.

Grandpop died one night right in the middle of dinner, said Tony, at the house in the mountains. That's the way to do it. No sickness, no pain, no warning, just keel over into the spaghetti and that's the end of it.

Grace remarried a few years after the divorce, a man she knew from work named Rodney Fell. Tony first met him the day Rod took them on the train to visit the 1965 New York World's Fair; in his eight-year-old mind, the exuberant joy of that afternoon, the cotton candy and indulgence and his mother's giggles, set the mood for the subsequent change in their family structure. Mild, calm, and even-tempered, Rod was the antithesis of Eddie. There was a famous family story I heard many times about Tony's younger brother Frankie getting caught jumping on the roof of Rod's beloved green Rambler convertible, and Rod just asked him not to do that again, if he didn't mind.

Though Tony's father never would have allowed Rod to adopt the boys legally, Tony's transfer of allegiance was complete. Frankie, who remembered less of the bad times, continued to yearn for his father, even after Eddie was remarried to the woman he'd dumped their mother for and had new children and the boys were second-class citizens on their weekend visits. I hated going there, Tony said darkly. I hated that bitch he married. I just wish I never knew him in the first place.

Tony was not like most people these days, who seem to come complete with ready-made self-analyses explaining how they have or have not overcome their dysfunctional pasts. He just had stories, sometimes fragments of stories, which I fit together like pieces of a torn-up letter, flattening out the scraps and taping the ragged edges, reading and rereading to figure out the missing words. It was a way of loving him, of making his past mine.

Of his skating career, which was essentially over by the time I met him, I have images in my mind so clear they seem like my own memories, though they are really a mishmash of things he told me and photographs I saw, like the snapshot of the ten-year-old with blond bangs and big brown eyes zooming across the pond, his green scarf and his younger brother trailing behind him. He is repeating the magic words of the TV commentator to himself: double lutz, triple toe loop, flying camel. His feet know something he does not.

A few years later, he started lessons at a rink an hour from their house in Lansdale, to which his mother chauffeured him every morning before dawn, then sat in the stands in her thick red coat reading a romance novel. His coach hovered nearby as he traced the slow curves of the school figures over and over until they were right, the scraping of his blade the only sound in that huge empty space.

Tony was not yet beautiful at sixteen. As if he had stepped into his reflection in a circus mirror, his legs and arms were too long, his hair was too long—it was, after all, 1973—his nose and even his ears were too long. But on the ice, the fact that he really was too tall to be a skater gave him an unusual sort of elegance. That was the year he left home and went to Lake Placid to train. His gift for footwork and choreography, spreadeagles and spins, the intricate stepping and crossing and gliding that are most like dance—these stylish moves won him a medal in Junior Men's Regionals. His idols were Hayes Alan Jenkins, the Protopopovs, Dick Button, young Misha Petkevich, and above all, Dorothy Hamill, who was also training at Lake Placid at that time. He went as often as he could to watch her practice, transfixed by her layback: that deep backward arch, neck extended, head dropped back, arms moving upward with the languid grace of plants underwater.

When he moved into a jump, every part of him was pure concentration: gathering momentum, pushing off his edge, lifting into the air, spinning once, twice—Yes! shouted the girls as he landed it. All the girls from his boardinghouse were crazy about him, his wisecracks, his record collection, his green packages of Newports. They made him sit in their rooms as they curled their hair and mended their skating costumes. They loaned him their acne medicine.

But he needed more jumps, more triples, more athleticism in his performance to move up in the rankings. His coach added a double-triple combination to his program and the fall was so hard when he missed it, he didn't even like to practice it with other people around. He had nightmares about those falls, the shock of flesh and bone smacking into ice.

No, he couldn't do it, it was too much. In competition, awake for days from nerves, nail chewed, eyes rabbity, he missed his jumps, flubbed easy moves, couldn't skate the way he had just yesterday, goddamnit. He tried all the tricks, the mantras, the Valium, sessions with a hypnotist. It didn't work. He kept telling himself it didn't matter, he didn't care, and soon he began to believe it. Anyway, he was too tall to be a skater. He had started too late. It cost too much money. So fuck it.

His coach saw what was happening and found a way out for him. He arranged for Tony to go down to New York to audition with Holiday on Ice. Tony was ecstatic when he was accepted in the chorus line of one of their European touring companies. He loved playing the Road Runner, loved the sequined costumes and gaudy sets, the other kids in the company, the channel crossings and hotel rooms and last-minute rushes to the train station.

He acquired a taste for Pernod, Dunhills, and other duty-free luxuries. He learned to do beautiful laundry using only a bathroom sink and a balcony rail. He could buy poppers in many different languages and became very graceful at letting other people pick up a check.

He loved to tell about the time a little boy in the audience in Hamburg ripped off the Road Runner's head during the part of the show where the characters skate through the audience. Give me back my head, kid! he hissed urgently. Give me back my goddamn head! Wile E. Coyote whizzed past, snatched the head, and flew to center ice. The decapitated Road Runner chased after him, laughing, ice flying from their blades.

They fined us half a week's salary, he said. God, those fines! If you had one loose button on your costume, if you were a minute late for a rehearsal, if you were spotted in performance without a wall-to-wall smile on your face for even a second—we got so many fines we used to worry we were going to end up owing *them* money.

At the end of Tony's second year, his company moved to the Far East, first stop Taiwan. But the very first week, while they were moving the show into an arena, he dropped a wooden container full of props on his foot. When he failed to recover after six weeks in a British hospital, he was sent home.

By the age of twenty-one, he'd become a coach at the rink in New Orleans, standing on the ice in a nylon jacket with a silver whistle around his neck watching his little girls trip over their feet. For four years, he choreographed their programs, agonized over their costumes, squired them to competitions in distant cities, and brought home their trophies. They loved him, the parents loved him, he was so good, so patient and kind, but somehow it was not enough to keep him from slipping away. He rushed into the arms of his downfall, like Judy, like Liza, like

Jimi and Janis, like the rock and roll heroes and art stars we all grew up worshipping.

And that was when he stopped calling his mother, I finally figured out. When he lost his job and lost his kids and lost his balance and he just couldn't bear for her to know how hard he had fallen.

THE FLOOD

For three months in the late spring and summer of 1983, Tony and I lived on the second floor of a slave-quarter apartment on the corner of Royal and Ursulines in the French Quarter. You came through a passageway off the street, across a courtyard and up a flight of stairs into our kitchen, which had red brick walls and polished wood floors and a very high window through which a shaft of light slanted down at a lovely sharp angle over our appliances. It overlooked the courtyard of a guesthouse for gay men, and bits of gossip and details of meals at Galatoire's drifted in with the sound of splashing water from their hot tub. Sometimes I would find Tony standing on the stove, spying down.

The only other room contained a blue corduroy fold-out couch, a nonworking fireplace, and a small desk bearing an aqua-and-white Smith-Corona at which I wrote and rewrote the opening paragraphs of the last story for my M.F.A. thesis, "Heroin Girl," a fictionalized account of my last days in New York. Long drapes of heavy crimson moiré covered the windows and the French doors leading to the balcony. There was not even room for a dresser; we kept our clothes in a cupboard in the bathroom.

What I remember most clearly about the few months we lived in that apartment was the flood. New Orleans is famous for its floods, and the best place to be during one of them, the highest ground, is the French Quarter. Since we were not only in the Quarter but on the second floor, we really had nothing to fear from the rain itself. We saw doom and destruction on television, houses and cars floating down the street, people going to the Canal Villere in canoes, but we were high and dry.

I repeat, high and dry. Only not high enough for me to gracefully endure being trapped in a tiny apartment for three days with a man who was now driving me to the brink of lust-induced psychosis. With the couch folded out into a foam pad on the floor, our living room was not much more than a bed and, with the red drapes drawn and the rain pouring down, there was nothing to do but lie in it. There was no place else to go except the kitchen or the balcony, the latter of little use in a hurricane. So we lay in that bed in our underwear for three days watching the flood on TV.

And he would not touch me.

I tried every trick in the book. I tried sexy looks, back rubs, foot rubs, I tried walking around naked. I tried masturbating in front of him. I tried getting him drunk. I tried talking dirty. I tried crying, pounding my fist, and other histrionics, as well as both asking nicely and begging. I even tried the educational approach: I drew him a little diagram of the female anatomy, explaining where orgasms come from and even why girls get their periods. I swear, he did not know this. That's Catholic school for you.

I would try to draw him out, ask about gay sex. He said big dicks hurt less, not more. He described postsex toilet patterns. Shyness wasn't the problem, and talking about gay sex wasn't the answer. The problem was that most of the time he just tuned me out, sitting three feet away reading a magazine without looking up, as if I weren't even there. Occasionally, he got angry, throwing down the magazine and stalking off. What the hell do you want from me, Marion? he said. Sometimes at night he would talk in his sleep, garbled rants of which I could understand nothing except that he was not at peace. Well, I wasn't either. The more he ignored me, the more obsessed I became.

When I think back on this phase of our relationship, I don't know how I lived through it. Not that I didn't eventually learn to get by without much sex, but certainly not while maintaining this depraved frame of mind. Could you direct me to the nearest brick wall, sir? I just want to bang my head on it. Please just keep rejecting me, it makes me so hot when you do that.

Ultimately, we made love on five or six occasions while we lived in the Quarter, each an improvement over the last and a cause for great celebration on my part. But the sad fact is, no matter how I would have wished it, sex was not one of the main activities with which we occupied ourselves in those early months of living together, and working didn't take up much of our time either. Tony had quit the Calf before he left for New York and did not bother seeking new employment upon our return. I taught a night course at the local SHKEC outpost, but that required no more than a few hours a week. Not sex, not work, not political activism or exercise or cooking, no, we had no time for such frivolous pursuits. We were too busy getting high. As long as I still had money in the bank and he still had masses of change in his wooden salad bowl, drugs were what we did during those golden early months. The merging most new lovers achieve with their bodies, we accomplished with our chemically altered minds.

I never did figure out where to buy heroin in New Orleans—and believe me, I tried. Nobody knew. Or at least nobody would tell me. I went so far as to look for accounts of drug busts in the *Times-Picayune,* then visit the neighborhood of the crime and walk up and down the block in a sundress. The only way I could figure out to get dope was to have Nancy and Steve send us some via Federal Express, which I did at least weekly. On the days the shipments were expected, I would take a folding chair and a pack of cigarettes downstairs to the sidewalk in front of the house and wait. Sometimes it would be 10:29 before that damn guy showed up.

Since that wasn't enough by itself, we got into the drug of choice of the gay residents of the Quarter, crystal meth. As it too could be injected, it at least satisfied my needle fixation. And talk about a rush. It's a cymbal crash in your head and veins and guts, a reverberation that seems to go on forever, a sudden chemical taste in the back of your mouth, and Hey, I've got an idea! Let's reorganize the silverware! We'll play some records! Look, here's a book on origami! Remember origami? Come on, let's go to the bar and drink!

Ah, yes, the bar. Make that bars, plural. There was the good old Bourbon Pub, and the Bistro and the Loading Zone, those were our dance places. It never ceased to drive me crazy that they wouldn't let me into the men-only Jewels or Café Lafitte in Exile. Though actually, one Halloween years later, Tony and a friend of ours in heavy drag and I in some costume that covered less than 10 percent of my surface area were attacked by a gang of macho assholes right outside the door of Lafitte's and the doorman noticed, intervened, and pulled us inside. Finally! I don't know what I had always expected to see in there, but that night it was a roomful of guys dressed as nuns.

For the nongay nondisco alcohol experience, we had the Blacksmith Shop, Coop's, Mississippi Riverbottom, Blondie's, and the weirdly crooked, profoundly smelly Blue Crystal. When we went to places like these, Pete and Shelley would sometimes meet us, especially if there was a cheap happy hour with free food to help justify the expense of not drinking at home. Pete and Shelley were high-functioning alcoholics-on-a-budget; they had no interest in drugs. They were like an aunt and uncle to us, the most normal influence in our lives.

They came down to the Quarter every Tuesday morning for

the $1.99 breakfast special at La Bohème, a run-down little coffee shop with red leatherette booths where the Joe Cocker–Jennifer Warnes rendition of the theme song from *An Officer and a Gentleman* might just as well have been the only song on the jukebox. *Lift us up where we belong, where the eagles fly, on a mountain high.* I fell perversely in love with this song; the bald waiter Curly and I worked for months on our imitation.

But as for speed, no matter how much fun it was at the outset, it always ended in hell. I have never experienced despair of the kind that flooded over me as the meth wore off, every cell in my body depleted, my brain an aching cavern with suicidal thoughts rushing to fill it, talked out, walked out, danced out, half-poisoned from alcohol, exhausted beyond belief but unable to sleep.

Sometimes it was so bad I couldn't even bear to be around Tony. I would go to the park and stare at the sidewalk, but even that hurt my eyes, which could not stand to look at anything anymore but would not close. The only things that could get me through these periods were (a) knowing it would go away eventually, (b) finding someone with Valium or other downs, or, better yet, (c) getting some dope from Steve and Nancy. Sometimes we would cleverly remember to place our order in advance.

Toward the end of our life in the Quarter, we finally got a new hobby, a less dangerous and more durable one. VCRs had just become more widely available and reasonably priced, and Tony convinced me to ask my parents for one for my twenty-fifth birthday, which coincided with my turning in my thesis, faking my way through an exam about Virginia Woolf's *To the Lighthouse,* and receiving the highly valuable degree of Master of Fine Arts in Creative Writing. Dear old Dad sent a check for five hundred bucks right down.

Since the video craze was new, the closest store that rented movies was out in Metairie, which was, incidentally, the site of the only good place to buy bagels. So we'd drive out to stock up on movies and bagels once a week. We both loved movies: old movies, new movies, good movies, bad movies, anything.

We had a Judy Garland festival one weekend, for which one of Tony's fellow Judy-freaks loaned us his collection of tapes and Tony pulled out his many coffee-table books, paperback biographies, and reference works on his idol. *A Child Is Waiting, The Clock,* and *A Star Is Born* were his favorites from the Garland film archive. Since my relationship with Judy had begun and ended with *The Wizard of Oz,* I had a lot to learn.

He lectured to me about the importance of each film in her career, exactly how messed up she was on drugs at that point, where things stood with her and Vincente Minnelli, the trajectories of the subcareers of daughters Lorna and Liza. Judy was his anima, his romantic heroine: child prodigy, androgynous beauty, openhearted diva of vulnerability, her colossal talent and sense of humor locked in a fight to the death with her self-doubt and tragic excesses.

Our decadent French Quarter lifestyle could not last forever. By June, my money-market account with its eight thousand dollars was soon to be history and Tony's salad bowl was empty. The SAT courses didn't pay enough to live on. Then one night Tony ran into an old friend who had moved to Austin to run the skating program there and offered him a job. Yes! I said. Let's go.

We had each lived in Austin before. Tony had been there for only three months, during the summer, during his Juan period, in a dumpy apartment complex near the mall on the northern edge of town—one or all of these, I argued, were the reasons he hated it so much. I had fallen in love with Austin when I visited with a college friend over spring break in 1976. It was a gorgeous green paradise full of Mexican food and frozen drinks and cowboy hippie types playing rock and roll. I had lived there for three years after college in a little house full of dogs and people—Nancy and Steve had met at a city pool there, and six of us East Coast transplants shared a two-bedroom place in the groovy Clarksville neighborhood—before I made the gross error of moving to New York. A return to Austin would be, for me, a homecoming. Just the thought of driving into town on I-35, the Key Motel coming over the wide Texas horizon at the northern city limit, made my heart leap. I knew I could make Tony love it too.

Up to this point, I had still been half-thinking of going to law school in either Berkeley or Boston, but Austin sounded like much more fun. I saw that any interest I'd thought I'd had in going to law school was a drug-induced hallucination and mailed off letters requesting a one-year deferral. I never thought seriously about the subject again. My parents, who had seized eagerly on the law school plan as evidence that I was finally going to shape up and do something reasonable with my life, were crushed. They had practically sent out a press release when I was accepted at Harvard. Now I was throwing it down the drain—because, my mother pointed out, of that goddamn gigolo!

But little did I care to hear any of her opinions. I was going to be a great writer, and Tony was going to support me teaching ice skating. So there.

By this time, I was looking forward to leaving the French Quarter, as life in a gay ghetto was no longer any fun. Once I had admitted the truth of my intentions toward Tony, I could no longer play fruit fly. I felt excluded and oppressed by my surroundings. Jewels and Lafitte's had the right idea: it was no place for a straight woman.

Exacerbating these feelings was the fact that half our neighborhood was composed of people Tony had once slept with. Both they and the other half were eager to reexperience or newly discover the magic. Every time I turned my back, some guy would be chatting Tony up, buying him a drink, fondling his leg.

One night I came out of the ladies' room (well, not the ladies' room, those bars never had ladies' rooms, but sometimes you could at least find a stall with a door) and found him engaged in an extremely passionate-looking, lengthy, and highly French kiss with some guy I'd never laid eyes on. I just stood there and stared for a minute, making sure I was really seeing what I thought I was seeing.

Fuck this, I said as I stalked past him, out the door of the club and back to the apartment. There I reduced both kitchen chairs to splinters by slamming them against the refrigerator, the floor, the walls. Tony wandered in shortly after and we had an argument that ended with his climbing out on the roof to escape my wrath.

I climbed out on the roof after him, which scared him to death: if anyone is uncoordinated enough to fall off even a fairly flat roof, it's me. I was scared too, and immediately lowered myself to a sitting position, sliding myself away from the eaves. Tony hesitated a moment, then walked over and knelt behind me. I didn't turn my head, though I could feel his breath on the back of my neck. The June night was humid and thick, the purplish sky starless; the asbestos scraped the backs of my legs through my thin summer dress. Then he put his hands on my shoulders to anchor me, and that broke the tension. Both of us were crying.

All that shit you've told me about how you felt about what Juan did to you, I said after a while.

I know, he said. But really this was no big deal, Marion. It was a stupid kiss and a stupid person and it was nothing.

I would feel better if we could have a little less of this particular nothing, I replied.

I don't know what made me think I had the right to say this, the right to demand fidelity from someone who didn't even share my sexual preference, but somehow I did. And Tony wanted emotional security so badly that he accepted it in return for the same loyalty pledge. We were about to become the most monogamous, joined-at-the-hip, virtually asexual couple on earth. And have many happy years doing it.

In sunny, sexually diverse Austin, Texas.

OZONE PARK

Nancy and Steven had decided to get married that July, so we had to detour back to New Jersey on the way from New Orleans to Austin. We needed clothes for the wedding, a present, a U-Haul, and some speed to get us down all that interstate. By this point, I was well into my credit cards and loans from my father. Tony had a few hundred bucks from his mother, with whom he was finally back in touch, thanks to my constant nudging.

All right already, I'm calling her! he said one day. I was so excited, I made the uncharacteristic gesture of leaving the apartment to give him some privacy. His reconnecting with his family was important to me for selfish reasons as well as altruistic ones. By calling his mother, Tony would acknowledge that his life had changed and that I was an essential part of its new incarnation.

While we were up on the East Coast, he took me out to meet his parents and brothers; Nancy and Steven were to come up and join us later in the weekend. Grace and Rod were at their weekend place in the Poconos, one of two houses on Lake Wallenpaupack his grandmother Ida, widow of Valdrick, had bought for peanuts many years earlier. After what seemed like hours on narrow, heavily wooded roads, Tony finally pulled the Civic into a gravel driveway beside a split-level red cedar bungalow. As we climbed a flight of steps to the screened porch, a short, wide woman came to greet us at the door.

You finally made it! How was the traffic? Nice to meet you, Marion, said Tony's mother in a high-pitched, Philadelphia-accented, girlish voice that would have been less surprising com-

ing from an animated bunny than from this little tank of a person
with thick black eyebrows stretching almost uninterrupted over
her coal black eyes. She hugged her son and took his suitcase.

I put you in your old room with Sammy, Tone, she said.
Frankie and Larry are staying down at your grandmother's house
with their friends. Why don't you take Marion's things down to
the basement? Then you can walk down to the lake and see
everybody.

Rod, who had been reading a magazine on a patio lounge, got
up to smile, shake my hand, and utter a few monosyllables. My
own family was very kissy, but physical affection, I was to learn,
was rare and awkward in Tony's house, leading to a certain
strained offhandedness about arrivals and departures.

I was not happy about the idea of sleeping apart from Tony.
We were grown-ups, after all. We were living together. Hadn't I
personally rescued him from homosexuality and God knows
what else? Not to mention having been instrumental in his finally reestablishing contact with his family after a period during
which, Grace told me later, she thought something horrible had
happened to him, even considered he might be dead? I was not
going to put up with this. But Tony and his mother were already
going inside with the suitcases, and she was chattering away
about the plans for the weekend. Rolling my eyes at her back, I
followed them in.

"Weekend place in the Poconos" sounds much fancier than
the house really was, a prefab bungalow most memorable for the
extensive collections it housed. In the living room alone were
Grace's figurines, souvenir spoons, snow-domes, and music
boxes, as well as piles of mail, newspapers, comic books, and pa-
perbacks aging like wine. Putting things away and straightening
them up, much less actually cleaning, did not appear to be high
priorities in this household. I was no neatnik myself; I couldn't

have cared less. But I could not imagine how Tony, whom I knew as an absolute fanatic for domestic order and spotlessness, a person who did not go to sleep without Windexing the kitchen counters, had ever lived there.

Then I remembered the stories of his father hitting his mother for not tucking the corners on the sheets tight enough, not polishing the faucets in the bathroom, not waxing the floors. If she never picked up a mop or broom again, if she never bought another can of Ajax, I realized, Tony would not hold it against her. Nor would he acknowledge that anything was awry by doing it himself—though in his own house, he cleaned as if expecting his father any minute.

Tony's homecoming dinner was a full-fledged feast; his mother had prepared every one of his old favorites. Even an ordinary dinner at Grace's included enough dishes to fill the menu of an Italian restaurant, but this time she had outdone herself. We had antipasto, stromboli, bragiola, Italian sausage, meatballs and spaghetti, as well as salad, broccoli, beans, garlic bread, and two kinds of pie with ice cream for dessert.

As I would see over time, it was not just Grace's food that was impressive, it was the organization behind it. Everything she made turned into something else; various components were prepared ahead and actually improved during their stay in the refrigerator. There were no leftovers, only works in progress. It was as if she had cruise control in her kitchen; once she got her momentum going, all she had to do was steer.

Crowded around the long picnic table in the kitchen were the cast of characters I had been so eager to meet. Tony's stepfather Rod was a man of few words and many martinis; I was with him on the martinis, at least. His extreme diffidence made it difficult to get to know him, though I knew it was an aspect of the gentle spirit that had endeared him so deeply to Tony. Still, I swear I never saw the two of them have more than a minute-long conversation. The majority of their interaction consisted of sitting in adjacent chairs, reading.

Tony's brother Frankie was a slightly shorter, heavier, regular-guy version of Tony whom I took to right away. He was into smoking pot and listening to heavy metal; he had a sweetness and a silly sense of humor quite like Tony's. Their little half-brother Sam, Grace and Rod's son, was only about fifteen at the time, a cute loudmouthed kid. There was a foster brother, Larry, a kid from their neighborhood in Lansdale whom Grace had virtually adopted and raised as her own when his family fell apart. Each of the older boys had a girlfriend and a few miscellaneous other guests, but feeding an army of people was something Grace had no problem with. My own mother would have had a fit.

After two cocktails and a few glasses of Italian red with the meal, I loosened up and cracked what I suppose I intended as a joke. So Grace, I said, I bet you didn't make them stay in separate rooms when Tony brought home his boyfriends.

Since I knew the family had never acknowledged or discussed Tony's gayness and that any boyfriends who had visited had appeared under the guise of garden-variety chums, I should have been aware that my comment would not exactly pave the way for a jolly round of repartee. Indeed, after a moment of silence during which only Frankie made eye contact with me—the expression on his face clearly said, Girl, you are nuts—everyone immediately started asking for things to be passed to them and commenting on the food.

This is ridiculous, I said when the two of us went out on the deck afterward to smoke a cigarette. I'm not sleeping by myself.

Will you calm down, he said. Just sleep in my room and Sam will sleep downstairs. She won't say anything.

He was right. She didn't.

The next day, we all sat out on the Astroturf-covered dock drinking gin and Wink from Tupperware glasses. Grace pronounced it "Tubberware." She had a gift for completely innocent but often wonderful malapropisms: grapes were picked by migraine workers, packages delivered by United Partial Service. As the afternoon wore on and the level of gin in the bottle dropped, our conversation took on an increasingly loony quality. Meanwhile, more aunts and uncles had arrived, as well as Tony's grandmother Ida, a tiny Italian matriarch with a self-effacing little-old-lady demeanor and the will of iron to go with it.

Like her late husband Valdrick, Ida was a family character about whom Tony loved to tell stories. She was a devout Catholic, but the Vatican's position on divorce had given her problems. Her daughter Grace had been excommunicated after divorcing Tony's father, as had two of her other children after their own misbegotten marriages. Ida had despised her sons- and daughter-in-law and was certain that Jesus was with her on this. There was no way He intended to expel her children from His family for expelling such lowlifes from their own. She undertook a letter-writing campaign to various Catholic dignitaries, starting with the local bishop and continuing straight up to the pope, until she somehow had them all recommunicated.

Only Grace among the siblings deigned to be welcomed back to the fold, but one had the feeling it was more because her mother had gone to all that trouble than for any other reason.

Ida was sweet to me, though her initial attempt to make conversation left me bewildered.

Did you ever know Sister Mary Joseph or Sister Sophie? she asked. They're old friends of mine.

Um, I don't think so.

Well, I just thought you might because they're from Ozone Park.

Really, I said politely. It began to dawn on me that someone had told her I was from Asbury Park, a town in New Jersey, and she had confused it with Ozone Park in Queens.

Oh, yes, she said, and they teach at a wonderful convent school, St. Ignatius. You must have heard of it. Everyone in Ozone Park knows St. Ignatius.

No, I said, I'm from Asbury Park, and I'm Jewish.

Oh, she said. That's nice. Which church did you go to?

A muffled chortle issued from Tony's direction.

My sister and Steven arrived on Sunday and seemed to my paranoid eye to be greeted much more warmly than I. Probably since they were about to be married, they were officially assigned to share a bed. Nancy was a basket case; the wedding was in two weeks and she hadn't even decided on a service. She'd brought a huge pile of books she'd checked out from the library about alternative ceremonies, but found something wrong with every one of them. She wanted me to help her write something from scratch, which was going to be a chore, since while she had no problem ruling out the unacceptable, she had no idea what she did want.

Okay, Nancy, let's just put something down and then we'll fix it up, I said cheerfully. Stop crying! Don't worry! We'll take the good parts from the Native American and combine them with the modified Unitarian, maybe add a poem or two from Kahlil Gibran.

Aside from her agonies about the ceremony, and her dress, which she insisted made her look fat, and dozens of other problematic details, Nancy had serious doubts about how our family and Steve's would get along. The two sets of parents had never even met in the six years she and Steve had been together, and there was a good reason for this. Our parents were college-educated upper-middle-class Jewish golf and bridge players. The Cerbos were first-generation working-class Italian-Americans; his father, alternately a barber and a school custodian, could barely write in English. The Golf Club Family and the Chip-on-Their-Shoulder Family. *Goodbye, Columbus* meets *Rocky*. Just picturing them all together in one room made Nancy feel ill.

Steve and Tony went out water-skiing and left Nancy and me to our travails, hunched over a spiral notebook on the deck. At one point, I went in to get us some iced tea. Grace was in the kitchen fixing lunch.

My poor sister, I said. She really doesn't know what she wants.

That's completely normal, Grace replied protectively.

I know that, I shot back, having expected a little commiseration, and anyway, who was she to be protecting my sister from me? I'm just trying to help her, I continued defensively. That's what she came up here for, so I could help her.

Well, don't push her too hard. You'll make her a nervous wreck.

She already is a nervous wreck! I'm not making her a nervous wreck!

You can't expect to come up here and take over, Marion. A wedding is a personal thing.

I took a deep breath and and exhaled sharply through my nose. No matter what I said, Grace took the opposing point of view. She hated me, I could tell.

Two weeks later, Nancy and Steven were married at my parents' golf club. In the many photographs taken the day of the wedding, the grass is insanely green, the sky ungodly blue, and, in the distance, the small red flag on the eighteenth green lifts in the ocean breeze. There's a shot of Tony on the brick steps of the clubhouse: he looks like a CIA agent in his dark wraparound

Ray-Bans, loose-fitting jacket, and slim black pants. But it's not the clothes, really, it's his way of hovering at the edges, checking everything out, rarely getting involved but missing nothing. When Tony left a party, he would always know what everyone was wearing, whom they spent time with, how drunk they got, who took them home, what kind of car they were driving. Years later, he would point out a pair of shoes: Look, those are the same pumps your Aunt Joyce had on at Nancy's wedding.

Tony did much better with my family and their crowd than I did with his. Everyone liked him; he was good-looking and charming and debonair. Despite a few minor problems—the minister skipped a whole page of our carefully wrought ceremony, Eddie Gonzalez absconded with most of the coke we'd bought for the reception, and it turned out an aunt of Steve's had been in the ladies' room eavesdropping while Nancy and I were getting high in the next stall (The bride and her sister are drug addicts! she ran out to report)—the wedding was a raging success.

Nancy looked beautiful that day, her blue eyes and blond hair and white-toothed smile so dazzling that any supposed flaws of the dress were imperceptible. My father was at the top of his form: king of the golf club and all he surveyed, putting on the party of the year. My mother and I stood watching the two of them dance to Frank Sinatra's "Nancy with the Laughing Face," and I remembered how jealous I used to be because there was no song like that for me, only "Marian the Librarian" from *The Music Man,* and it was nowhere near as romantic and Marian wasn't even spelled right.

I felt none of that jealousy now, though my little sister was getting married first and this was her big day. Really, it was our day: I was her maid of honor, and she had involved me so much in the planning that I felt personally responsible for how well it was coming off. I too loved Steve, and was as excited about his being my brother as she was about his being her husband. And lest that give way to a tiny green-eyed flicker, I had my own personal gorgeous Italian boy at my side, so there was nothing to be jealous of.

Pete and Shelley were up from New Orleans and his band, Wild Kingdom, played a few numbers late in the evening. The Ali Family got out there and danced the way we always did, me, Mali Wali, shaking my butt and hips, Nali shaking her shoulders and tits, Stali all funk and shuffle, and Beau Tali gliding magically across the floor.

LOVE NEST

Who needs hard drugs when you've got Austin in July, a central nervous system depressant as powerful as any ever sucked into a hypodermic needle? The normally laid-back population of the Texas capital slips in summer into a citywide swoon. Laziness, procrastination, and most varieties of decadent behavior are broadly indulged; swimming and napping in particular are elevated to acts of civic solidarity. To lure the sagging natives to work and jump-start their discharged brains, the office buildings have their air conditioners set to subarctic levels. In restaurants, at weddings, even at church socials, margarita machines churn. Insects show who's boss, and like a population under siege, the humans stick together, especially if they make the mistake of touching each other. Despite the absence of key elements like a communal mess hall and an archery range, Austin does a decent job of impersonating a large-scale, all-ages summer camp.

From my first bite of migas—scrambled eggs with fried tortillas, peppers, onions, cheese, and ranchero sauce—my first glass of iced tea, my first plunge into the vast, gorgeous city pool at Barton Springs, I could hardly believe I had ever moved away. The simplest pleasures, like driving my car to the grocery store and not having it towed away or leaving my house unlocked and not having it robbed, were a thrill to me after New York and New Orleans.

Yet Austin was not quite as small a town as it had been when I'd first encountered it in the seventies. By the time I left in 1981, a real estate boom was transforming the center of the city and stretching its borders. Though the boom was decried by many for ecological, aesthetic, and spiritual reasons, upon my return I did not find the city changed in essence. It had always had a colossal ego, like the rest of Texas: for me, raised in a state with a self-esteem problem, this was part of its charm. Neither the boom nor the subsequent bust did much to change the inhabitants' view that they were among angels, living in heaven.

The change in the local economy had one unfortunate effect: my old neighborhood just west of downtown, Clarksville, was now far too expensive for our reduced fortunes. So me and my baby got us a little shack on Jeff Davis, the most famously named of the namesake streets that ambled through the unaspiring north Austin neighborhood that fell into our price range. The other streets nearby paid homage to citizens of more mysterious renown, Jim Hogg, Joe Sayers, Mssrs. Koenig and Ullrich, each now loaning his arcane glory to a bedraggled Boulevard or Lane. Everything about this run-down neighborhood with its shaggy, stunted greenery spelled R-E-N-T. Few home-improvement projects pitched further than a couple of weeks into the future were undertaken by its residents, a quintessentially Austin mix of footloose students, upward-striving young couples, and old folks who had been there since the dawn of time. Though I never made any friends in that neighborhood or even learned many people's names, Tony knew exactly who lived where and would comment on any divergences from their usual patterns of comings and goings.

Our house was a white clapboard box divided into four rooms, featuring once-beige carpeting, pitted linoleum, a single space heater, no AC, and ceilings so low that the outlandishly tall landlord could not stand up straight when he came to visit. Its star attraction was its extremely low rent, a key requirement at this point. When we arrived in Austin in August, essentially penniless, the teaching job Tony had been offered evaporated like spit on a sidewalk. His friend never even returned his phone calls.

I was frantic about this. How was I going to become a great writer if he didn't have a job? I kept urging him to go over to the ice rink and find the guy, but that required a kind of assertiveness Tony was incapable of.

It wasn't that Tony had a problem expressing his opinions. When adequately provoked, he could be fearsome in his vehemence. Once while entering an intersection in Manhattan, he was cut off by another driver, a pointless move since it was rush hour and no one was going anywhere but gridlock hell. Tony slammed the car into park, jumped out and spat on the guy's windshield. I expected to see him mowed down by machine-gun fire right then and there. Another time, I found a half-written notecard stuck in a book he was reading, addressed to a friend who owned a Mexican folk-art shop near our house. Dear Marcia, it began, I just had the worst shopping experience of my life thanks to that dopey cow who works at your store.

But when it came to agitating to get something he wanted, like the teaching job, Tony was Mr. Wait-and-See. I had no patience with this approach. Like an obsessive high school guidance counselor, I was determined to inspire him, egg him on, or force him into more achievement-oriented behavior.

As the phone call continued not to come, we speculated that this old friend of Tony's couldn't handle the idea that he and I were a couple. He had betrayed his gay brethren; he was out of the club. Not every gay male friend reacted this negatively, but practically all of them were at least somewhat bemused by the situation, made more confusing by the fact that Tony never claimed to be a bisexual. He was a gay man who happened to be in love with a woman—who had forsaken all others to make his life with her. It was an odd choice and, for some gay friends, a threatening one—a kind of mixed marriage.

And what was it for us? Here we were, two people who would later joke that if we invited all of our respective ex-lovers to our wedding we would have to rent a convention center, and we had each chosen a partner with whom we were less than compatible sexually. Had we just had enough sex, or at least enough of sex being the most important thing? A convention center full of disappointments later, had we just developed other priorities? That must have been true for Tony, who became a virtually asexual being once he fell in love with me. I, however, actually believed that our physical relationship would eventually work out the way I wanted it to, and failed to consider what life would be like if it didn't.

Part of why I had fallen in love with Tony was specifically because he was gay: off-limits, impossible, forbidden. To be with me, he had to change his whole life, and the idea of someone doing this on my account appealed to me deeply. I needed it. It was as if I were partially deaf, and someone was finally screaming loud enough for me to hear. I was a drama queen—the part was made for me. At least since Judy Garland wasn't available.

For Tony, who, despite his natty appearance and carefree demeanor, was really falling apart at the time we met, a changed life probably didn't sound like a bad idea. And maybe I did remind him of Judy Garland, at least a little. I certainly had the excess, the vulnerability, the spotlight-snagging, onstage approach to life. He used to joke that he fell in love with me because I carried a whole carton of cigarettes in my purse.

More than lovers, we were like infatuated grade school best friends who spend every waking minute together and never tire of one another's company, experimenting with sex occasionally at wild sleepover parties. My need for attention and closeness was one Tony was fully capable of filling. He never got sick of me, never wanted me to go away, never needed to be alone. He could be alone with me around just fine, with his head in a magazine or taking a nap. When I required more than just his physical presence, he came right back, sometimes a little grumpily, but back. Finally, I was not too intense.

Nor too wild. No stupid things I said or did when I was drunk or otherwise fucked up were ever a problem. I acted like a jerk last night, I would say, remembering some inebriated poetry reading or raunchy break dance.

No you didn't, honey, he'd say. You were funny. Everyone loved you.

What we both wanted, deep down, was the security of unconditional love, the no matter what you do, no matter what you say, I will always be right here. Even if you're gay and I'm straight. Even if you're beautiful and I'm just okay. Even if I have money and you don't. In fact, we melted into each other. I gave him money, he taught me how to dance. I made him smart, he made me beautiful.

And beauty had so much to do with it. I loved being with Tony and being seen with Tony because he was so beautiful. His beauty and his love of beauty were not superficial; they were him, they poured out of him. Within a month after we moved in, he had completely glamorized our pitiful shack with fifties furniture from thrift stores and tchotchkes from Mexico, making a dumpy cracker box with formerly beige carpeting into house beautiful. Even the bathroom had voodoo candles, postcards of the Virgin of Guadalupe, a basket of colored soaps. There were Bunny Matthews New Orleans cartoons pinned up on the wall surrounding the toilet and a hanging plant flourishing over the tub. To me, fixing up the bathroom meant putting in a new roll of toilet paper; I was truly amazed.

While Tony was redoing the house—he even went so far as to build and stain a worktable for my typewriter and papers—I put the great writer thing on hold and got a job writing technical manuals for a computer software company, a position I ended up keeping for more than a decade. In my spare time, I reactivated my connections in the local literary scene; soon there were plans for what would be my second small-press book, illustrated by Sandye, Steve, Shelley, Pete, and few other artist friends. I received a call from a woman named Liz Lambert asking me to read in the series she emceed weekly at a café downtown. Liz, a smart, funny blond lesbian with a heavy West Texas accent, was one of the first new friends Tony and I made as a couple and became a central figure in the close circle we eventually assembled. In those early days, we would visit her in the red brick duplex she shared with her gay twin brothers, staying up half the night drinking and talking.

Eventually, my sweet Beau Tali ran out of walls to paint and had to find something else to do. Skating was out. How about something with flowers? Clothes? Music? Hair? We decided his future one night when Nancy and Steve were visiting and we were all high sitting by the edge of Town Lake shouting out possibilities like we were playing *$25,000 Pyramid.*

Beauty schools and liquor stores were the two main types of business on the decaying retail strip that bordered our neighborhood, so it was a simple matter for Tony to sign up the very next day at the Modern College of Hair Design. For nine months, he set off for school every morning on his bicycle wearing a beautifully pressed white shirt and a pair of jeans, carrying his lunch in a paper sack under his arm.

The Modern College of Hair Design was run by a prissy, self-righteous born-again Christian couple named Gordy and Viv. They were all preachy and smarmy and love-thy-neighbor on the

surface, slave drivers and Scrooges underneath, gleefully collecting money from everyone who walked in the door. The clients
paid to get their hair cut and the students paid to cut it. What a
deal. Gordy and Viv's downfall was the fact that their outlook on
life made them seriously at odds with their trendy young student
body.

Tony hated them on principle from the outset and over time
developed a genuine loathing for Viv, who had a sugar-coated
voice, a Doris Day flip, and absolutely no mind of her own. Now
here was a dopey cow if there ever was one. Within a few weeks
of his enrollment, Viv and Tony were at war over what music
should be played on the school's sound system. She set the radio
to a Christian Muzak station; every time she walked out of the
room, he'd run over and change it to the black station or college
rock. Then he started bringing in cassette tapes from home,
compilations he made of bands like the Smiths and Dead Can
Dance and Tears for Fears.

One day, Viv returned from lunch to find Boy George rock-
ing her world and she had had enough. She minced over to the
tape deck, ejected the tape, and dropped it in her purse. Tony
looked up from the squirming six-year-old whose hair he was attempting to cut, dropped his scissors on the back bar, and strode
over.

That's my tape, said Tony.

You can pick it up after five at the front desk, she informed
him, clutching her purse as if he might grab it away from her.

Inspired by her gesture, he snatched at the purse. That tape is
my property and I won't be here after five, you fucking bitch.

You certainly won't, said Gordy, a meaty hand on Tony's
forearm.

By the time he confessed to me that he'd been expelled from
one beauty school, he'd already been across the street to enroll

at another, Gordy and Viv's prime competitor, the actual name of which I can't remember since Tony always referred to it as the Postmodern College of Hair Design. The Postmodern College was run by a jolly, laid-back guy named Ranger Ronnie who was perfectly happy to have the kids blast their music and dye their hair purple. Word filtered back to Tony's friends in Christian boot camp, and by the end of the month three-quarters of Gordy and Viv's students had transferred.

People had a way of clustering around Tony, of following him. It was not just that he was a trendsetter; he was fundamentally a good person to be around. He enjoyed hanging out so much, drinking coffee and smoking cigarettes, that his pleasure in it was contagious. You couldn't help hanging out with him.

That fall, the newlyweds, Nancy and Steve, moved back down to Austin from New York for a while, trying to clean up in the drug department. Some dealer friend they'd been sharing a loft with in SoHo had just gotten busted, and his girlfriend had ended up on the Bowery hooking, and the whole ordeal threw a major scare into them. Of course, once they arrived, they started ordering FedEx shipments and on the days one was expected, we'd all be on the phone to each other all day to see if it had come. We'd meet at their little house downtown after work and shoot up and talk and laugh and play cards and dance to Steve's rap tapes. Eventually, we'd have to go home and we'd lie in bed, too high to sleep, drifting over the whispering plains of the subconscious in a waking dream.

Do you want to get married? Tony asked me one night as we lay in this state.

What a great idea, I said. Let's get married and have some babies.

I couldn't wait to tell my mother.

Anybody don't want their sugar? asked a black girl, poking her head in between Nancy and me. We were cross-legged on the cement floor of the cell, dispiritedly looking through the contents of the lunch sacks the jail lady had just wheeled in on a cart.

You got any cigarettes? Nancy asked her.

I do! said a skinny older woman behind us. You still got your sugar? You want to trade?

Why do they all want the sugar? I whispered to Nancy after she had completed the negotiations and we were puffing on a pair of Kool 100s.

Junkies, said Nancy. Sugar craving.

An officer came into the corridor and read a list of names, but ours were not among them. We'd been in jail overnight, but already I felt totally swallowed up, as if we might be there for the rest of our lives. I had no idea what was supposed to happen, when, or in what order, and there were no opportunities to ask questions. We had been taken to the precinct by our arresting officers, then down to Central Booking in a van, chained together with a dozen other women, slamming into each other on every pothole and turn, and now to wherever the hell we were going to await whatever the hell it was.

Down at the precinct, before we were separated from Tony and Steve, we had been arguing about whether to call my father. Steven was totally against it. He said with the amount of dope we had, we were too small-time for the Manhattan criminal justice system to bother with. We're gonna walk, he kept saying. Leave your poor father alone.

You'll walk, agreed some wizened expert on the bench across from us, polishing the one remaining lens in his horn-rimmed glasses. Beside him, a huge bald fellow with a baby face unselfconsciously played with himself through his pants, grinning. Cut that out, you, said the older man, slapping his hand.

I didn't want to take any chances. Tony had a prior arrest, a marijuana charge up in Lake Placid. Steve had "walked" earlier that year after being picked up on Avenue C; how could he be sure he'd get so lucky again? Meanwhile, I had meetings scheduled all the next week at my office down in Texas, I was already going to miss my plane home, and definitely could not entertain the prospect of a prolonged incarceration. I had to close on my new condo, for God's sake.

So at eleven-thirty on a Sunday night, I called my father to tell him that both his offspring and their respective gentlemen friends were in the custody of the law and could he please do something?

And Thanksgiving weekend at my parents' in New Jersey had started out so nicely—Nancy and I in the kitchen helping my mom, Tony polishing the silver and setting the table, Steven fixing the broken screen door, my father, as usual, sitting at his computer working, a football game blaring in the background. The weather was perfect, cold and clear, the sky cloudless. We kept taking the dog for walks just to have an excuse to be outside, the miniature dachshund shoulder-deep in leaves as she trundled along.

At dinner, the talk was largely of Tony's and my wedding, scheduled for the following June; with another big party to plan, my father and I were in our element. Tony and I were about a year into our initially half-joking engagement, but definitely weren't kidding around anymore. Several of our friends had gotten married since Nancy and Steve, and we'd sit there holding hands, listening to the service and the vows, glancing into each other's dewy eyes during the kiss. We too wanted to stand up in front of everyone wearing beautiful clothes and say those words, make those promises, have that tender embrace. We wanted everybody to know how much we loved each other, always and forever, and to drink and eat and dance with us all night long. Then wave goodbye and get on a plane to Jamaica.

I once read that nothing is more boring than other people's happiness. A wedding is one of the moments in a relationship when that happiness can be less boring, can open up and become an exciting collective event. That's certainly what I wanted—to share my joy, to say, Look, can you believe this?

After the wedding, the next item on my agenda was having babies. I was twenty-six, and over the past two years had gone from ignoring infants completely to commandeering them whenever possible, holding their heat against me, feeling the weight of them on my shoulder or hip, so natural it was like a memory. Tony had taken a while to warm up to the idea of children, but probably only because as a gay man he'd never considered the possibility. Once he did, it wasn't hard to talk him into it. He was made to be a father. Or at least a mother. He was incredibly good at taking care of both people and things. Thanks to his instinctive solicitousness and gallant domestic attentions, even our houseguests were so well cared for they never wanted to leave.

Well, all these big plans were on hold at least until we could get out of jail. I couldn't believe how stupid we were.

We had been doing drugs all weekend, sneaking off to Nancy's old bedroom on Thanksgiving Day, in the car on the way to Philadelphia to see Prince the next night, back in Manhattan at Steve and Nancy's apartment in Washington Heights. Sunday night we'd gone down to the Lower East Side to stock up for a last hurrah before our flight home the next morning. Once we'd scored, there was an argument over whether we should drive all the way back uptown to the apartment or just pull over somewhere. Tony and Nancy wanted to drive home; Steve and I were the impatient ones, and also the more dominating, so we ended up on a side street in Stuyvesant Town, cooking up the dope in the handy bottle caps Nancy carried with her at all times, along with her jar of water, Q-tips, and syringes.

How could we have known that this particular neighborhood was in a state of emergency due to a psycho rapist who had been rampaging through the area? Hundreds of eyes peered down at us from under raised window blinds as our unfamiliar car pulled into the street outside. Scores of fingers dialed the police to report an intruder. And before anyone except speedy Steven had the chance to get a needle anywhere near his or her arm, a half-dozen police cars screeched in and blocked the car on all sides.

They quickly determined we were not the psycho rapist. We were the usual bunch of kids in a car with Jersey plates, come into the city over the weekend to score. They seemed to assume the white powder in question was cocaine, and we never bothered to enlighten them.

Now my sister and I were packed into a cell with a dozen other women, nodding out, talking to themselves, arguing with each other. I was trying to act brave for Nancy, but I was terrified. I couldn't believe I was locked up in this little room and couldn't go anywhere or do anything or call anyone or even find out what was in store for us. I had gotten no sleep the night before, lying on the cold, dirty cement floor under the never-turned-off fluorescent light, my stomach churning, my mind racing. I could have been a political prisoner in Argentina for how intensely I felt the loss of my freedom and how desperately I doubted the immediacy of its return. For a worthless thing like getting high, I had given up control over my life, not just in some larger sense but on a minute-by-minute physical level. Every decision from whether I could go to the bathroom right on up to if and when I could go home was now in the hands of the Authorities, who didn't know me or care about me, who were arbitrary and angry and faceless and bureaucratic.

I kept thinking, Nothing is worth this. I will never let this happen to me again.

We had been in jail for about twenty-four hours when suddenly, late Monday night, things started to move very quickly. We were reunited with Steve and Tony and hustled onto a bench in a huge cathedral-like courtroom. A few drug-possession cases were heard before ours, each with a defendant who had clearly been around this block before, and Steve shot me looks as each did indeed walk.

When our case came up, we were pleased to learn that we had a lawyer—a well-dressed black man not much older than we were who introduced himself as a friend of my father's and who had gone to law school with the judge's son. Like everyone else, he seemed to find it slightly comical that all four of us had managed to wind up in this predicament together. Your father is here, he told us, and he's pretty pissed off, but we're going to save your silly asses anyway. This time. Next time you want to go on a double date, try a movie.

He asked Tony a few questions about the old marijuana charge, approached the bench, and shortly after, we were free.

Our charges had been dropped to a misdemeanor possession

of paraphernalia, we were fined a hundred dollars each, and the records were permanently sealed.

My father was, as reported, pissed. I didn't tell your mother about the needles, he said. You're a bunch of goddamn idiots. Let's get something to eat.

We adjourned to a steak house with candles in sconces on flocked velvet walls, where we ate like pigs, drank red wine, and regaled each other with jail stories, laughing so uncontrollably the unincarcerated air might have been nitrous oxide. Afterward, my father drove Nancy and Steve home, then dropped Tony and me off at the airport.

For God's sake, Marion, he said, you're too old for this. I'm too old for this.

I know, Daddy, I said. I'm sorry.

He looked so tired, his usually ruddy face pale and the circles under his eyes dark and deep. Drive carefully, I whispered in his ear as I kissed him goodbye.

We got the next plane out, and I was home in time for my Tuesday afternoon condo closing—and even had the down payment, thanks to my father, who again rescued me, loaning me the three thousand dollars I was short at the last minute. You're sure there's really a condo, he said, you're not buying crack or something?

I had planned to tell everyone at the office some bullshit story about the airport being snowed in, but the truth was so bizarre and ridiculous that I ended up confessing it in detail to at least a few of my coworkers. Though I emphasized the funny parts for their benefit, and my own as well, the feeling of being locked up without an option in the world clung to me like dirt from the cell floor.

I never enjoyed writing installation instructions or thinking up catchy headlines to sell C compilers as much as I did that first week back at my desk. All I wanted was to go to work, cook dinner, get married, have babies, and try to be a decent person in the world. I had so much—too much to risk losing it all for a few meaningless hours of artificial euphoria. It was time for me to grow up, while I still had the chance.

THE WEDDING

Tony and I were married on a Sunday morning in March 1986. Reagan was still president and the space shuttle had blown up that January, but these misfortunes and other, more personal ones did not make a visible dent in the mood of the event, preserved on video by my Uncle Barry, a professional cameraman for the NBA.

We are so in love, Tony and I. The expression that crosses my face during the ceremony, a kind of amazed joy, is so strong it looks almost like caricature. I look as if I've won the daily double, or have been overtaken by the Holy Spirit and am about to fall down on the floor and begin speaking in tongues. Tony holds his emotion inside him better, but his dimples deepen and his eyes brighten and he squeezes my hand so tight.

Though Steve and Nancy, the best man and matron of honor, are swaying a little, Tony and I are perfectly straight, as I had intended when I set the ceremony for 11:30 A.M. I was so serious about this that I had spent three days in abstemious seclusion at my mother's house—I told everyone I was "getting my virginity back"—while Tony led the party contingent through pre-wedding debauchery in New York.

Tony is wearing a gorgeous black zoot suit we bought at Parachute in SoHo (my mother felt compelled to wonder what was wrong with the still-controversial Kenzo). His hair is cut in a flattop; his face is scrubbed and eager—he gives the impression of being a young man from a more innocent time. He stands by his mother and stepfather in the receiving line, all three of them beaming. The Heubach–Winik merger was going more smoothly than the Cerbo–Winik one had, thanks to the less extreme class differences and greater goodwill of the parties, ready and eager to be united around the concepts of an open bar and our future happiness. Grace and Rod had thrown a party themselves the night before, driving in from Philly with a vanload of lasagna and chocolate cake.

I am in ivory lace, a two-piece tea-length ensemble with peekaboo cleavage that moved my grandmother to comment with feigned outrage, "She looks sexy!" The dress had been purchased by my father well over a year earlier; it was the last thing he bought for me in his life.

Less than two months after our release from jail, I was back in Manhattan, keeping a nerve-racking vigil with my mother and sister outside the coronary care unit of New York Hospital as my father underwent triple-bypass surgery.

Sitting for three days in that ungodly quiet waiting room with a few other families, waiting our turn for the good news or bad news that arrived at random intervals on rubber-soled shoes—Mrs. Bradley? Bradley family? Could you come this way? and your heart would clench for the Bradleys, whom you would never see again, and one of those times the nurse would be coming for you—I couldn't help but wonder if the stress of our stupid escapade had had something to do with the heart attack that occasioned the operation. I had taken my father's strength, his resilience, his bullheaded good humor and perennial savings of the day for granted all my life. The sight of him half-conscious, pale and helpless, cut open and roughly sewn back together was hard to accept.

In fact, though he made it through the surgery and was sent home to recover, my father never seemed completely himself again, an edge of exhaustion tempering his brashness even as he raged against his frailty. Forbidden to go back to work full-time, he nevertheless spent hours on the phone with his employees. He became obsessed with the golf club, spearheading a massive modernization and redecoration of the clubhouse and supervising its execution in minute detail. Suppliers and decorators pleaded with the club president to get Mr. Winik off their cases as he tested every piece of kitchen equipment, checked out every computer program, and insisted no carpet be laid or curtain be hung until he came by to approve. It was said that he even tried on the waitress uniforms before authorizing their purchase.

During this period, he began calling me more often than usual, fretting about one thing and another. One day in late March, he reached me at work to talk about something he said he'd been thinking about for a while.

The drugs, he said. You, I'm not worried about. It's your sister. I'm concerned about her.

Why only her? Why aren't you worried about me? I answered, always the competitive sibling.

Oh, you'll be fine. Just watch out for Nancy, he ordered.

Okay, I said, but how?

I don't know, he said. You figure it out.

With me, he was more concerned about finances than drug abuse, calling with questions about my condo mortgage and advice about my tax return. He insisted that I open an IRA.

On April 4, 1985, he failed to appear at a House Committee meeting at the club. The committee members sent someone over to the house to check on him.

My mother returned that afternoon from a short trip to Florida, where she'd been visiting her best friend Nancy Kimmel, taking a break from the rather intense phenomenon of my father, the semi-invalid. When she got off the plane and saw her sister Joan and not him waiting for her, she knew instantly what had happened.

Down in Austin, I was home from work with an immobilizing pain in my lower back I had never experienced before, but which has since become chronic. It was unusual for me to miss a day of work, it was very unusual for me to take a Valium, and most unusual of all to go to the Sonic Drive-In and pick up a chili dog for lunch—I was a vegetarian—but the way the day was going, I just gave in. Pete and Shelley were visiting at the time, helping us break in the new apartment. That particular day, they were catering to my sudden invalidism, waiting on me hand and foot so I wouldn't have to get up. I was lying in the master bedroom with the miniblinds drawn, gently propped up with my chili dog, when my sister called and said, I have bad news.

How bad? I asked, my teeth suddenly chattering.

Bad, said Nancy, bursting into tears. The worst.

Half-hysterical with grief, I threw a black dress into a straw bag and went to the airport, thinking I would never stop crying or even want to.

There was some talk, among the dozens of family members and friends who hung around my mother's house in New Jersey for a week after the funeral, drinking and eating—they called it sitting shiva, without a hint of irony, as if we were covering mirrors and rending our garments—that Tony and I should go ahead and get married as scheduled that June. These shiva-sitters said it was Jewish tradition not to reschedule a wedding because of a death. I couldn't picture trying to have a party just two months later. I couldn't picture even talking about it. What with the radical reinterpretation of Jewish tradition in full swing at our house that week, I saw no problem with postponing my marriage.

Tony was an absolute angel during Shiva-Fest, as he called it, endearing himself to everyone, including my mother. From morning to night, he fixed drinks and washed dishes and emptied ashtrays and ran errands and moved soiled tablecloths through the laundry cycle. Nancy and Steven's main contribution was a package of dope they had shipped to themselves from Chiang Mai during their trip to Thailand. It had, with perfect timing, just showed up. My job was to talk to people, but the only conversation I remember was when my grandmother's sister came up to me and said in her stagey red-lipstick way, You have to be strong, dear.

The thought that I had to be strong was almost more horrible than anything else. My grandmother, who was fixing herself a cup of coffee, who had had to be much stronger than is remotely reasonable on this and many other occasions, turned and said, Oh, leave her alone, Ethel.

But Ethel was right. I did have to be strong. I knew damn well that no one would ever again take care of me the way my father had; my mother, certainly, did not subscribe to his school of mollycoddling. Without him, I was no longer a child; I was my own last resort. And everything that had made him such a hero to me—his magnanimity, his open-mindedness, his vehemence, his unique combination of irascibility and humor, his insane capacity for work, his ways of taking care of people, forever giving them rides, finding them jobs, and doing their tax returns, usually yelling at them all the while—all that I had left of it was what I could manage to find in myself.

The day of the wedding, almost one year later, we fit ourselves around the absence of my father. He had okayed the carpets, he had bought the dress, and we had to make do with these souvenirs of his love and good taste. My mother and grandmother escorted me down the aisle, Mommy in an ivory damask suit, Gigi in huge black and white polka dots and the dark sunglasses she always wore for her eye problem. In the video, Gigi is mainly seen approaching the camera to ask my Uncle Barry, the cameraman, if he's had anything to eat yet.

Please, Barry. A little something. Try the smoked trout.

Meanwhile, my uncle cannot take his eyes off his ex-wife, my Aunt Ellen. It is heartbreaking how his camera lingers on her, then he catches himself and quickly pans away. Watching this on my television nine years later, I know we are all just this stupid and pathetic, nobody realizes what they have before it's too late, nobody loves anyone as much as they do once they've lost them completely.

My uncle is dead, my grandmother is dead, Roddy and Junior and Nancy Kimmel and Charlie Klitzman and Myra Cohn and Carol Jacobson are dead, and that is just the beginning. Where there is not death, there is divorce, there is change, there is drifting away, until a world once solid and full of possibility is torn apart, depopulated, so drastically rearranged it no longer exists. All those sweet wishes for health and happiness, those sincere promises of faith and permanency—goddamn daisies under the steamroller of what happens.

For many, the most unforgettable moment of the wedding was just before our first dance, when we entered the dining room together and the deejay announced us: And now . . . Mr. and Mrs. Winik!

Whispers swept the hall. Everyone was sure the deejay had made a mistake. But no, Tony had decided to change his last name to mine. "Heubach" belonged to the father he so despised; if it had been up to him, he would have become a Fell when his mother married Rod. His attitude made things simple, since I had no intention of changing my name. I had no brothers and my father was dead; I hoped my children could be Winiks.

I might as well have the same name as my kids, Tony told people. By this time, we talked about these hypothetical kids of ours as if they already existed.

I loved the idea, loved how people reacted to it, and, yes, loved what it said about us. I was the man of the family. Tony was mine.

My groom and I danced our first dance to Tina Turner's version of "Let's Stay Together." We twirled like kids on a playground, forgetting all the slick moves we had practiced for months, mouthing the words at first, then kissing with abandon. The next song was David Bowie's "Modern Love," and the dance floor filled up with our friends in their sequins and mohawks, as well as Tony's mother and Uncle Buddy and grandmother Ida, and from my mother's group, Charlie Klitzman, a lawyer with a wooden leg who had given me my first summer job. Everybody else watched with a combination of disbelief and glee, like it was the Moscow Circus.

Later that evening, I fell asleep sitting at my father's old desk in his padded swivel chair with my mother's dachshund curled up in my lap. Tony was entertaining hangers-on in the next room. I would have to lose my recaptured virginity some other time.

RESULTS

Surrounded by our two sets of china, our crystal and flatware and linens and Calphalon pots, wearing our fresh Jamaican suntans, we returned from our honeymoon to resume domestic life in the little condo among the treetops of Clarksville. My software company was doing well; I was now in charge of advertising, packaging, and trade shows as well as technical writing. Tony was an increasingly sought-after hairdresser, working late several nights to accommodate all the people who wanted him to cut their hair. With two incomes and good prospects, we had left our funky shack on Jeff Davis behind and returned to my old favorite neighborhood at the beginning of 1985, a few months before my father's death.

This turned out to be the peak of the real estate boom that had covered central Austin with Southwestern-style stucco condominium complexes like bluebonnets in the hill country in spring. By the time we were married, values had plummeted so drastically that our place was worth half of what we'd paid for it.

But so what. We loved it there. The location was idyllic: a grocery store, a Mexican restaurant, a twenty-four-hour Minit Mart, and an old-fashioned pharmacy with a soda fountain were all in walking distance. Our conjugal paradise was hidden on a quiet intersection up a saltillo-tiled flight of steps, and featured a bedroom and bath on either end of an L-shaped living and dining area with a narrow kitchenette. It was small but lovely, with wooden fans hanging from the cathedral ceilings, lots of windows, trendy wallpaper, and pedestal sinks in the bathrooms.

The walls and carpets and counter were all silver-gray, our furnishings black and turquoise. Tony was in his antiwood phase; even our dining table was a smoky shade of purple-blue formica, with matching upholstered banquettes on two sides. It was perfect with our new Italian pottery plates.

One Saturday afternoon that August, I pulled the trusty Civic into a parking spot outside Avant, the stylish in-with-the-in-crowd salon where Tony worked with a bunch of other young fashion mavens maintaining the extravagant hairstyles of mid-eighties Austin night crawlers. Big hair for big minds, as they used to say. At the time, I myself was sporting waist-length extensions in a shade known as eggplant. I banged open the glass door of the salon and rushed back to Tony's station waving the Baggie that contained evidence of our success in the endeavor that had captured our attention all summer.

Tony hardly had to look at its contents, only my face, to guess the news.

Yes! he said, and our palms met in a high five. We're having a baby, he told his client, grinning hugely. Quick, somebody get me some—what is it again?—oh, yeah, get me some cigars. No, that's later. Get me some champagne. Taittinger, please. You can't have any, he told me, then stopped babbling and wrapped me in his arms.

The preceding summer, I had read the results of a different medical test in his face. It was called the HTLV-III test at the time, and it indicated the presence of antibodies to the virus that had begun to cause an epidemic of disease and death among gay men, IV drug users, and hemophiliacs. Prompted by the growing alarm of the reports he'd been reading in the papers and word of the first death in his old French Quarter crowd—Joseph, the other bartender at the Golden Calf, a dissolute fellow with a great, bitchy sense of humor and a rasp of a voice to go with it—Tony went to a doctor as soon as the availability of the test was announced in 1985.

I was sitting at the purple dining-room table watching his face through the pass-through to the kitchen when he made the call to get the test results. He wasn't speaking, so I couldn't tell if someone was talking to him or if he was on hold. His expression didn't change at all. Then suddenly he said, Thank you, in a quick, strained voice, hung up the phone, and lit a cigarette from the one he was smoking.

Bad? I said.

He gave me a dark look and went out the front door.

Since we had been having what would soon be known as "unsafe" sex, not to mention sharing hypodermic needles for more than two years, my test would surely be positive too. I went down to the city health department to have my blood drawn under a false name the city assigned for purposes of anonymity—mine was Betty Seven. Against every expectation, Betty tested negative.

Shortly afterward, my sister and Steve were tested too; again, he was positive and she was not. It was more surprising that Nancy and I were unscathed than that Tony and Steve had been infected. Tony, after all, had come of age as a gay man in the late seventies. His sex and drug history fit the AIDS profile to a tee. He figured he had been positive for at least three years at the time he was tested, probably more, since he had not been involved sexually with anyone but me since we met but there had been quite a parade of partners before that. Steve, though unwaveringly straight, had been shooting dope since high school, ages before anybody thought anything about sharing needles, and he too had an old buddy who was dying.

We had these test results nine months before our wedding, but the fact that Tony was positive didn't make me not want to marry him or have his children. I figured that if everything we'd done so far hadn't given me the disease, why would a few more milliliters of semen be any different? The fact that my sister too was negative despite repeated exposure indicated to me that perhaps we shared some kind of immunity. I knew that if I didn't get the virus, my children wouldn't either, since transmission to the fetus occurs during gestation, from the mother's blood. I could get tested during my pregnancy to make sure my "immunity" had held up; as long as I stayed negative, the baby would be fine.

The long-term possibilities—that Tony would get sick, even die, that I would then be a widow and a single mother—had no reality to me, no power. Except for the results of this blood test, and his by-then perennially swollen lymph nodes, he was radiantly healthy. It was 1985—early, for AIDS. Not so many people had died as to make a bleak outcome seem inevitable. I thought there would be a cure. I thought there would be exceptions. I thought things would be fine.

I used to think everything would be fine. I used to sit on people's deathbeds and think everything would be fine. My optimism was not only relentless but infectious; for a while, Tony shared it with me. Maybe he believed that I could shape the future by sheer force of will. It was an impression I was good at giving, since I had trouble disbelieving it myself.

HTLV-III or no HTLV-III, I had decided it was baby time. And how do you make a baby? You have sex! Sex without rubbers! What a thrill that would be. The need to use condoms, which Tony despised, had had a negative impact on our spotty sex life, which I was by then sort of used to, but sort of not.

Nobody but us thought trying to have a baby was such a good idea. Not Tony's doctor, not my gynecologist, not my mother. Tony's mother didn't get to weigh in on the issue since Tony had decided not to tell her about his test results; he didn't want to worry her. Faced with our determination, Tony's doctor suggested that he be tested to see if he was "shedding" the virus in his semen. The doctor explained that the current belief was that carriers of the disease went through contagious and noncontagious phases, and that if we could ascertain that Tony wasn't currently shedding, we could proceed with less risk.

We went down to a research hospital in Houston, where Tony jerked off into a cup. Afterward, we met some hairdressers he knew for dinner, took ecstasy, and stayed up all night dancing. I was partying like my days were numbered, which they were, because I knew I would have to quit everything as soon as we started trying to get pregnant.

It was supposed to take a month for the culture to produce results, but about three weeks into it the lab called to say the specimen had been contaminated. So we got in the car and repeated the whole experience.

When they called to say the specimen had been contaminated again, we decided to dispense with further testing. Tony did not like jerking off into a cup, and Tony rarely did things Tony did not like to do. Meanwhile, I was ready. I was more than ready. I was staring wistfully into other people's baby carriages and had borrowed two years of back issues of *Mothering* magazine, a black-and-white publication out of Santa Fe that promoted the all-natural, cotton-diaper, breast-feed-until-high-school approach. And I was going to renounce all my vices any minute.

To minimize the risk of AIDS transmission, we had sex on a precise schedule, designed to coincide with my ovulation. I researched the matter extensively and tracked the activities of my reproductive system as if I were running a wartime intelligence operation. I charted every possible indicator—basal temperature, cervical mucus, dates of last menstruation. When the moment arrived, I worked it for all it was worth. We had sex five times in two days.

· After all these years of bitching about how we never had sex, I've lately begun to have flashes of memory—how he would hold himself up on his arms, how my palms fit into the indentations on either side of his butt, how his dark head looked down there between my legs. Tony always said that I exaggerated about how we never had sex. The problem was that when we did make love, I liked it so much that it just made me think about how we didn't have it enough, and how I could never get it when I wanted it. I always had to wait until he decided it was time. And there were very long periods when it wasn't time, and I eventually got used to that, especially during the nearly five years that I was either pregnant or nursing. But in the end, when I flipped out, the waiting, the many rejections, and the years of frustration were all I could remember.

My calculations paid off; we got it on the first try. I doubt there has ever been a happier pregnant person on earth than I was, or a prouder, gentler father-to-be than Tony. Someone had given me a bound "Pregnancy Journal," with questions printed at the top of each blank page to encourage writing, and my answers are almost nauseating in their exuberance. In response to "Was the news of your pregnancy celebrated in any special way?" I wrote, in violet felt-tip marker, no less: "All over the world, champagne and confetti were the order of the day. Bears rode down the streets on bicycles with ballerinas balancing on their handlebars. A holiday was declared in seventy-two countries and hundreds of telegrams of congratulation arrived at our door. Meanwhile, Tony and I ate pasta with pistachio pesto for dinner and sipped mineral water as the future bloomed in wet pastel colors before our wondering eyes."

No doubt about it, I was high on life. And nothing else, for about the first time in recorded history, or at least since the age of fourteen. At the dawn of Ovulation Day, I had given up all of the following: cigarettes, alcohol, recreational drugs, prescription drugs, over-the-counter drugs, caffeine, artificial sweeteners, food additives, and anything else ever reputed to have a negative effect on a developing fetus. I was serious. I had a tooth filled without novocaine. The amazing thing is, none of this was hard to do. I had believed I would make this change at this particular moment for so long, it had the quality of an automatic passage, like getting your first bra or being able to vote. I truly felt I had no choice.

Tony quit smoking and switched to decaf coffee in solidarity with me. Once I stopped buying wine, he drank very little— alcohol was never a draw for him. I was that way about pot. So except for his occasional joint, drugs seemed to magically fade from our lives. That phase was over.

To replace everything I had lost, I started eating my head off. I gained weight quickly, despite prenatal aerobics class and all our long walks. I wore a tentlike blue denim maternity jumper almost every day. I didn't care. I was fat and happy. We were living a cliché, but we didn't care about that either. Like generations of couples before us, we had personally invented human reproduction.

That Halloween we went to New Orleans to visit old friends. We were Sylvester Stallone and Brigitte Nielsen. Tony made a lovely Brigitte, I, a fairly beefy Sly. Everyone but me took acid that night, and I actually had a great time with them, like I was the counselor and they the giggling campers.

FIRST COMES LOVE

Marion and Tony sittin' in a tree, K-I-S-S-I-N-G,
First comes love, then comes marriage,
Then comes baby in the baby carriage.

So said the invitations I made for our baby shower the following spring. It was a soirée for sixty at our friends Scott and Lexanne's on a Sunday afternoon, people spilling from the house down the back steps across the yard under the live oaks, munching chips with hot sauce, treating their hangovers with mimosas or Shiner Bock as Kate Bush and Chris Isaak serenaded the assemblage, which included hairdressers in stunning dishabille, erstwhile hippies, aging punks, poets, programmers, professors, and all the members of a lesbian rock band. Only one baby was in attendance, little redheaded Sarah Mallouk in her stroller. She was Exhibit A: The Future.

We were calling our soon-to-be-born son Peewee, so Scott had gotten a life-size cardboard cutout of Peewee Herman and spray-painted a backdrop for it reading WELCOME PEEWEE WINIK in Day-Glo letters and glitter on black. Piles of presents had been laid on this altar; the guests formed a circle around us as we sat down to open them.

When it was over, we carted home the T-shirts, the nightgowns, and the onesies, the stuffed animals, the crib mobiles, the tiny Reeboks, the stroller and the bathtub, the towels and crib sheets and nursery monitors and Snuglis. Tony washed each article of clothing in Ivory Snow, as directed in the baby manual, folded them, and stacked them in the closet of the former guest room, which had now most definitely become the nursery. Sandye had been down to paint the walls with schools of fish, seahorses, and shrimp; the vaulted ceiling was the sky, featuring a kite and a hot-air balloon and not a single cloud. The crib was aqua, and the miniblinds on the big picture window beside it were exactly the same shade.

We had finished our Lamaze classes and signed up for diaper service; my overnight bag, containing a peignoir from my mother, a crystal from my buddy the cashier at the New Age grocery store, and a tape of relaxing music to listen to during labor Tony had put together for me—MALI WALI LOVE MUSIC, he had written on the spine—was sitting ready by the door.

Then one night, less than a week before my due date, a mid-wife friend who planned to be with me during labor came over for dinner. Tony wasn't there; Thursday was one of his late nights at the salon. While we were waiting for the quiche to come out of the oven, she asked if she could check the baby's heart tones. Just looking at her puzzled expression as she moved her feto-scope around my stomach, I knew.

Peewee never entered his room or slept in his crib. He had died inside me, days before he was supposed to be born. With no apparent cause, no warning, no sign at all, the little heart inside my enormous stomach had simply stopped beating. I didn't real-ize it when it happened, at least not consciously. I had heard that babies moved less as they settled down into the pelvis prior to labor, so a day or two could have gone by without movement and I wouldn't have thought it meant disaster.

I lay in the maternity ward, the white faces of my doctor and my husband swimming above me in the dimness. I wanted a

C-section, I wanted a laser gun, I wanted anything but labor and delivery, but my doctor said I'd have enough to recover from without getting cut open. I could go home, she said, labor would probably begin on its own within days.

I didn't have the slightest inclination to go home and wait, so she started an induction.

Whatever agony I went through during labor—screaming as the Pitocin-induced contractions tore through my guts, clawing at the belt of the monitor, demanding more and more Demerol, which they didn't refuse me but which only made me crazier because I'd fall into a druggy sleep and then be wrenched out of it by a contraction and have to remember what was happening all over again—what Tony suffered, sitting by that bed in a chair that I remember as doll-sized, helplessly watching, was just as bad. Maybe worse.

So geared up for something great to happen, all set to have the most wonderful experience of our lives, we had slipped into a horror movie, a gruesome mirror image of the happy script we had imagined in such detail. Like all the other mothers in the hospital, I was sweating and pushing and straining and crying, only instead of a cuddly baby, I would deliver a tiny, wet, perfectly formed corpse, with his father's big feet and his mother's dark hair.

When it was over, they said I could go home. Home. Great. It was torture to be there, with the ringing telephone and the silent nursery and the unbelievable emptiness.

The one saving grace was the kitten. Tony had gotten me a kitten for my twenty-ninth birthday, just one week earlier. This present was quite a surprise. I loved cats and dogs, but Tony had always said no pets, though we did have a cockatiel named Buzz, which I sneaked in under the wire. Somehow overcoming his entrenched aversion, Tony had secretly arranged to adopt one of the recently born litter of Depeche Mode, a friend's cat. When I came home from work that day, heard a faint mewing from down the hall, and opened the door of the guest bathroom to find a tabby kitten no bigger than my hand, I couldn't believe my eyes. Had he lost his mind? We were supposed to have a baby in a couple of weeks. How were we going to find time to pay attention to a cat?

That fortuitous kitten had a very lavish upbringing. If we could have put diapers on it, we probably would have. Rocco is eight now, as Peewee would have been. He is a good cat.

The day after I delivered Peewee, we had to drive out to a funeral home to make "the arrangements." The insane irony of being in that place instead of at home taking care of a baby was really too much. We walked in past a burbling fountain through rooms full of ponderous furniture and ritualized sympathy. We didn't hit it off too well with the director, who simply could not believe that we had chosen to name our dead son Peewee, that Tony had changed his last name to mine when we got married, or that we didn't want to pay extra to have a memorial service at his funeral home. We hated this guy, but we probably just needed someone to hate.

The autopsy had yielded absolutely no information: no cord problems, no placenta problems, and AIDS had nothing to do with it. The little dead boy was HIV-negative, and so was I. He was one of the twelve in one thousand babies who die shortly before or after birth for reasons no one can explain. Even so, there was some crap at the hospital about reluctance to handle the body of the son of an HIV-positive man.

My friend Dana and her boyfriend Paul were going out of town for a couple of months. They had a house out at Lake

Travis, a beautiful place thirty minutes west of downtown, and offered it to us as a way of getting out of our suddenly oppressive apartment. We escaped to the lake about a week after Peewee's delivery, and the first thing we did, lost and reaching for each other, was make love.

Minutes afterward, I felt a sharp jolt of fear. We weren't supposed to have sex for a couple of weeks because I was all torn up and raw inside from the delivery. And we hadn't used a condom.

I became absolutely convinced that I was infected. I had taken one chance too many; my luck had run out. This has happened to me several times over the years: in the wake of unexpected disaster, it's as if a lightning bolt causes my optimism generator to cut out and every grim possibility known to man rushes in to fill the dark. Suddenly, the universe becomes completely untrustworthy; anything could happen.

For years after that call from my sister telling me my father had died, I would tense up at the sound of a ringing phone, especially late at night or early in the morning. After a few misfortunes befall you out of the blue, you begin to live with a kind of low-grade dread, what I think of as Groundless Terror in Daily Life. If a friend is late, she's been killed in a car wreck. If you can't find the cat, he's been kidnapped by satanists. When your fear is so wide-ranging, so unfocused, no one thing that doesn't go wrong makes it better. It only shifts the focus. The friend, the cat, they're fine. So has the house burned down?

At least if you're worried about something in particular, as I was after Peewee's death, your fear can be relieved. I was still HIV-negative according to the test a few months later, and a few more months after that, and all the dozens of times I've been tested over the years.

About two weeks after the delivery, we had a memorial service for Peewee at sunset on a hilltop overlooking the lake. All those friends from the shower were there, holding hands in a circle as we lit candles and read a short elegy we had written. One line sticks in my mind: *We cannot let a place cleared for love be surrendered to bitterness and despair.* We played a tape of the Eurythmics' song "The Miracle of Love." The chorus of this song had become a refrain that played constantly in my heart: *The miracle of love will take away your pain / When the miracle of love comes your way again.*

To escape some of the awkwardness of this strange loss, we went out of town. We sat around my mother's house, then Grace and Rod's, then drove up to Shelley and Pete's land in the Adirondacks, where they lived deep in the woods in a little cabin they had built with their own hands.

We sat on rusty metal chairs around the stone fireplace in front of the house, drinking local jug wine. Pete cooked for us; Shelley presented us with handmade bark baskets and rag rugs and told silly stories. Though the isolation of the place was just what I needed, it was a little more glorious springtime than I was ready for, more wildflowers and baby birds and budding branches than I could bear to see. I kept my head bent over my knitting, a pastime I had taken up since Peewee's death with the relentless focus of a Madame Defarge. I knitted all through that trip, on the plane ride home and at our first social outing back in Austin, a big party Liz Lambert gave for her girlfriend's birthday.

By the middle of June, I had knitted a big red piece of nothing. I put it away and have not knitted since.

Toward the end of the Peewee "Pregnancy Journal," in the section labeled "Third Trimester," there's a question about sources of spiritual strength and support. My answer is "Tony, our relationship, our love, the ability to share with him all my ups and downs." Our marriage was the last thing I was worried about.

But in fact it was in the tiny, private universe between Tony and me where things began to go mysteriously awry. Some very bad scenes were played the summer after Peewee. Tony started acting weird: mulish, distant, and nasty. He was going out at night by himself. I'd call the salon and they'd say he'd left, but he wouldn't come home for hours. When he got there, he wouldn't talk to me. I was frustrated and lonely, and I couldn't believe with all the shit I was already going through, he was turning mean. It wasn't fair.

One night after dinner, I was in the kitchen putting away the leftovers. He was out in the living room watching MTV, seemingly half-asleep.

Tony, I called. Tony.

What, he answered irritably.

Come here.

What do you want, he said, standing in the doorway.

I want to know what you're doing. Where you're going all the time when you don't come home.

Out, he said.

What do you mean, out? Where? With who?

Shut up and leave me alone, he said.

No, I'm not going to leave you alone, I said, getting right in his face. What the hell is going on with you? Why are you doing this?

I was so shocked when he hit me. He had never done that before. I fell back against the refrigerator and instinctively kicked out my leg to make him move away. Maybe I hit him back, maybe he hit me again. I don't remember. I don't know if other people have this experience, but the memory of violence is like the memory of a dream, slipping out of reach before you can find the words.

I remember screaming over and over, My God, are you crazy?

I was lying on the floor crying when I heard the jingle of his keys and the door knob turning.

Are you going out again? I wailed.

Please, he said, in a thick, tearful voice. I have to get out of here. Just let me go.

That night I found a prescription pill bottle half-full of tranquilizers and another with sleeping pills. I waited until he came home and finally got the story—or at least part of the story—out of him. He was going around to clinics and telling doctors what had happened to us with Peewee. They were giving him this stuff to sleep, but he was taking it all day long. I suppose it was the only way he knew how to deal with his despair.

But it's turning you into a monster, Tony. Please, I hardly know you anymore. You have to stop, I begged him.

I'm sorry, Mali, he wept, totally undone. I'm sorry.

First comes love, then what? Comes pain, comes death, comes no nursery rhymes for you, poor baby, and there goes your empty stroller rolling off a cliff. It's just a shell game, after all—so sorry, too bad, you got the rock. The goat. The bomb. The empty space that sucks away your breath. Not the all-expenses-paid trip to Aruba but the jeering jack-in-the-box coming at you like a punch in the face. *Marion and Tony sittin' in a tree, S-C-R-E-W-E-D.* First comes love, then comes marriage, then comes this big fucking surprise called the rest of your life.

DREAM ACADEMY

I only knew one thing to do, which was to keep trying to get what I wanted in the first place. I wanted to have a baby. If we could just have the baby, I thought, everything would be all right. The doctor had advised us to wait a few months before trying to get pregnant again, but I couldn't see what good that would do.

For Tony's birthday in July, we went to Puerto Vallarta for four days. We stayed in a beautiful guesthouse run by an expatriate Texan, an older woman who had been a dancer in her youth. The guesthouse was a monument to her excellent taste and her close relations with the artisans and craftspeople of the area. The bathroom was Tony's favorite, all the fixtures hand-built from dark green tile, the deep rectangular bathtub the size of a small swimming pool. The bedroom, with its hand-carved four-poster draped in mosquito netting, was separated from the beach it perched over by latticework entwined with flowers. Fresh orange juice appeared every morning in the open-air kitchen.

Her son was visiting that weekend as well, a tall, thin guy with a droopy mustache and a sweet, funny face, staying on the top floor of the guesthouse. He had just lost his twelve-year-old daughter in a car accident. Our misfortune seemed to pale next to his. We had to cheer him up. We went out to dinner with him and his mother every night, ate sushi or steaks or Italian, then on for after-dinner drinks, going through pesos as if they were pennies, which they practically were. We spent so much time together in the course of those few days that the other locals assumed we were out-of-town friends or family. Though they were a godsend to us, and perhaps we to them, we never saw or spoke to either of them again.

I got my period while we were there, which depressed me a little. I thought maybe I would be pregnant already. I wrapped up the used tampons in toilet paper and stuffed them in the garbage can, not wanting Tony to know.

But I didn't have long to wait. By August, I was pregnant again.

This second pregnancy was very low-key in contrast to the first. We barely acknowledged it was going on until the third trimester. We didn't have to do anything—we had the room, the equipment, the birth plan, the pediatrician. We'd taken the classes. The never-opened overnight bag was still packed and sitting in the back of the closet.

By thirty-nine weeks, the week I'd lost Peewee, I was sick of waiting. Even my doctor was nervous, though the results from the fetal monitor tests she insisted I have every week showed the baby was fine. She offered me an induction, but I was set on natural childbirth and didn't want to be in the same room as a Pitocin drip ever again. I started trying folk remedies to bring on labor. I took long walks, tablespoons of castor oil, half-glasses of red wine. Despite the gymnastics required, we even made love.

The night our baby was born, we'd been to a Terence Trent D'Arby concert—I was swaying hugely from side to side, arms wrapped around my stomach, singing, *Sign your name across my heart, I want you to be my baby.* At home, we watched *Less Than Zero* on the VCR, then Tony fell asleep and I went out to balance my checkbook. I was having trouble wedging myself between the banquette and the table by then.

I felt a strange shift inside me, not pain, but slow-moving

pressure like a bubble rising, and eased myself up. As I walked across the room, a more intense sensation doubled me over, then there was an actual pop inside me. My water had broken; I was drenched. I ran in to wake Tony.

Relax, honey, he kept saying. Try to relax.

Relax?! I shouted. It's a little late for that.

We barely got to the hospital in time for Hayes to be born. In the mad rush that ensued, once again I didn't get to listen to my labor tape.

Swaddled in his blanket, wearing a knitted cotton cap on his little pink head, Hayes looked into our faces with calm wonderment as we passed him back and forth between us like children taking turns with a new toy. You've had him for a half hour already—hand him over!

He latched on to the giant breast I offered him like a pro, submitted peaceably to diaper changes and umbilicus swabbings, and even went to sleep when we put him in his cradle. The next day, he remained bodhisattvaesque as virtually everyone we knew came rushing to the hospital to see and hold him. The living room of our suite at the birth center was jammed with people and piled with take-out containers full of spring rolls and enchiladas, styrofoam cups of carrot juice, bottles of champagne.

We had magically reentered the state of bliss from which we'd been so roughly ejected when Peewee died. After months of dimness and drawn blinds, one gray room opening onto the next, after a long winter that was not as cold as it was quiet, now the sun streamed in the windows of our bedroom, falling in golden squares on our patchwork quilt, on the fluffy lambskin lining the cradle, on Hayes and Tony napping together, the baby curled against his father's arm. *Mali Wali's Love Music* was finally playing, filling the house with Dream Academy, Erasure, and the

Cocteau Twins. It was morning all day long, it was spring. The smells of clean cotton diapers and breast milk and soup on the stove filled the house. The three of us were in la-la land.

Tony had his own way of carrying Hayes, held against his hip facing out, secured by spread-open fingers curled over down around each leg. They'd cruise around like that for hours, a tall drink of water with his tiny baby. With his natural sense of costume, Tony had transformed himself visually into a yuppie Dad, had grown a ponytail and traded his contacts for rimless eyeglasses.

Except for nursing, there was no sex-role division of labor between us; Tony changed the diapers, pushed the stroller, did the laundry, and puréed the carrots as often as I did. Every night, one of us gave Hayes a massage according to the techniques we'd studied in infant massage class, then bathed him, sang him songs, rocked him to sleep. The innocence and sweetness of those routines was heady, irresistible. Hayes was a sorcerer; we were in his sway.

At first, the little magician came with me to work at the software company—I'd gone back part-time after just a few weeks of maternity leave, mostly because I was too hyper to stay home all day—until I got in trouble for nursing during business meetings. After that, Tony went part-time at the salon so he could be with Hayes in the mornings. No way were we going to put our precious one in day care, at least as long as we had the job flexibility to manage it; we never even got a baby-sitter until Hayes was almost a year old. I worked from 8 A.M. to 2 P.M., Tony from 3 P.M. to 9 P.M., then we'd eat a late dinner together and chitchat and watch TV.

By the time he was one year old, Hayes had seen all the Oscar-nominated movies (he was for *Good Morning, Vietnam*), had

been backstage at a Sade concert and in the third row for Tracy
Chapman. He'd breast-fed in all the finest restaurants, though
he'd made his weakness for low-rent guacamole known early on.
He'd won a Halloween costume contest for his interpretation of
the Last Emperor. He had been glued to the television with his
father as they cheered Brian Boitano to victory in the Winter
Olympics in Calgary. His travels had taken him to Mardi Gras in
New Orleans, the Jersey shore, Key West, and the Mexican state
of Oaxaca; he planned to celebrate his second birthday on the
Italian Riviera.

We became big experts on traveling with a baby. For car
trips, we had a lingerie bag hung from the back of the front seat,
each compartment stuffed with toys and treats. For plane rides,
we packed lollipops and juice boxes and individually wrapped
gifts to whip out in difficult moments. (Typically, I'd remember
everything but the diapers, then end up bumming them in air-
ports during layovers.) The slightest excursion required festive
preparations, as if it were Christmas, not just a ride in a car with
a baby. And it was not just traveling—everything was a fun project, a learning experience, a reason to make things and buy
things and read magazine articles and books.

One night on the road, driving up north for the holidays, we
stopped at a motel for the night. As we brought our suitcases
into the funky little room, Hayes asked, Is this a home, Mama?

Yes, it was a home. Everywhere was home (our place in
Austin he referred to as "the" home, as if it were an institution)
and everything was a party. We celebrated his six-month and
one-year birthdays, the day Tony and I met, the day we got married, each of our birthdays, and a half dozen other annual com-
memorations. Tony borrowed a video camera and shot endless
footage of the crawler and then the toddler. With his brown eyes
and blond hair, Hayes was already starting to look like his father.

My favorite photograph of the two of them at this time was taken downtown at the annual walk to raise money for AIDS. Tony is wearing a tie-dyed shirt, roller blades, cutoffs, elbow and knee pads. His long hair flies around his face as he pushes his miniature double down the street in a stroller.

By Hayes's second Christmas, I was pregnant with his little brother. Though I was still gung-ho with all my reforms, Tony had started smoking cigarettes again. I had suspected it for a while, but he just kept telling me it was pot I smelled, or other people's smoke in his hair. Puzzled, I kept snooping around until I found a pack of Newports in his jacket pocket while we were up at his mother's house for the holidays. No big deal, really, but I wished he hadn't hidden it from me for so long. His stepfather smoked in secret, or in "secret," since everyone knew exactly what he was doing when he locked himself in the bathroom or went out to get a paper or disappeared around the corner in the mall. Did we have to be like that?

Despite this disturbing development—as far as I knew, neither of us had ever hidden anything from the other before—things were still going pretty much according to plan. The plan included getting out of the condo, which was not set up right for a toddler and was far too small for the family of four we were about to become. The steps were dangerous, the fancy carpet was wrecked and the wallpaper was going fast. We needed a house; even more than a house, we needed a yard.

Unfortunately, the condo was still worth only half of what we'd paid for it. We'd have to rent it out and find a place to rent ourselves. Leaving the condo was inevitable but sad; so much had happened to us there. Tony had to paint over the mural in the nursery to make it look like a regular bedroom again.

What was definitely not in the plan for that Christmas of '89 was Nancy and Steve's breakup. But while we had been changing diapers and drinking carrot juice, they had become completely addicted to heroin. By the time things fell apart, they were spending a hundred dollars a day, ruining themselves financially, physically, and emotionally. Despite their frequent attempts to quit or at least cut down, dope had taken over their lives. When they finally shook free of it, they had nothing else left to hold them together.

I have had the amazing good fortune never to have been physically addicted to drugs. Though predisposed to party my brains out, I was an ambitious creature with big plans for myself. As much as I loved to get high, I was not going to totally fuck up my life. Every time I hit the downside of the drug roller coaster, my guilt, my sense of responsibility, and my self-concept would kick in, creating an internal limit that stopped me short of shooting up every day, burning my bridges, or exhausting my resources. The closest I came to self-destruction was right before I met Tony, when my despair over Jordan led me within a heartbeat of giving up on everything. But once I met Tony, I got my center back. I was doing drugs for fun again, not to kill myself.

Because of this, when I quit everything to become Mrs. Earth Mother, it was a spiritual craving I had to deal with, not a physical one, and the overwhelming experience of having and taking care of babies was a pretty fair replacement. But even though I had stopped doing drugs myself, I was still very attached to the idea of getting high. My appetite for altered states would never fully leave me; once I no longer perceived myself as the physical life source for my unborn or nursing children, the lust for that escape would surface with varying degrees of irresistibility. Even while ensconced in early mommyhood, I got a strange vicarious thrill out of talking to Nancy about their continued drug use.

Every time I spoke with her on the phone, I'd ask her about

it. She'd say, Yeah, we've been down a few times, and I'd ask her how it was, did they buy any coke, was it still so hard to get needles, should I go pick some up for them at the drugstore? She'd say yeah, yeah, yeah. But gradually she began to sound more desperate and I began to worry. I remembered my promise to my father, who had foreseen how things would go for us, and began to encourage her to quit. You have to stop, Nal, I told her, I'm really scared for you.

Whenever they left New York, it was with the intention of taking a break from dope. Even their move to North Jersey was partly an attempt to put some distance between them and the dealers. But each time they came down to Austin or met us somewhere, they would have increasing symptoms of withdrawal. They didn't feel well, they lay in bed or roamed restlessly around the house. Other miseries compounded the difficulties of these "vacations." One time Steve had shingles, which were almost certainly HIV-related; another time he'd brought just a little dope for everyone to try, then went swimming in Barton Springs with it in his pocket. To help with their withdrawal symptoms, I'd suggest acupuncture treatments or herbal tonics from the health-food store. When that didn't work, I'd offer my idea of less harmful substitutes.

At least, I'd say, have a little glass of wine. Smoke some of Tony's pot. Maybe we could find you a hit of ecstasy or something.

Nothing helped, except going home and starting all over again.

A month before, on Thanksgiving Day, Nancy had called to say she was going to check into a rehab center. They had gone completely nuts, were getting high every morning before work, meeting at lunch to get high, getting high after work, getting high behind each other's backs in between. Their track marks, the discolored lumps and bruises up and down their arms, were so bad they could only wear long-sleeved shirts in public. They were strung out all the time, exhausted, living for the one good half hour after each shot.

They had decided to make Thanksgiving a day off from drugs. They would stay home, make a nice dinner, build a fire in their fireplace. By noon, the plans had changed. Steve left for the city to cop. Alone in the house for hours, both desperate for and dreading Steve's return, Nancy fell apart. By the time she called me, she was so hysterical I could hardly understand what she was saying.

My mother was standing right next to me during this phone conversation, and after she'd finished talking to Nancy herself, I told her the whole messy story. She was shocked, all the more so because she surely must have thought she knew everything bad about us there was to know. I was never much for secrets; throughout our teens, my mother knew of most of our escapades whether she wanted to or not. But shooting dope? I never wanted to tell her about it, especially since it had started after we were supposed to be grown-up and done with wildness. Even my father, at the time of our arrest, had collaborated in keeping it from her.

So you were all doing—heroin? All this time?

Well, not all the time, Mom.

And Daddy knew?

A lot of people knew, Mom. Nancy Kimmel knew—she figured it out that time we all went to the Mexican restaurant near your house. Remember how Nancy and Steve were so late getting there and they were nodding out all over the place? Steven was always nodding out at dinner.

I thought it was because he was working too hard, she said.

But falling asleep because you're tired and nodding out because you're high don't look anything alike. (I gave her a little demonstration at this point.) Nancy Kimmel asked me about it later, that time we went to visit her when she was—so sick.

By this time, my mother's best friend Nancy Kimmel, a beautiful, kind woman whose blue eyes literally twinkled, but who had a salty streak you wouldn't expect from Mrs. Santa Claus, had died of a fast, deadly pancreatic cancer. My mother knew she was dying, but I, of course, sat there two weeks before her death telling her to eat brown rice and she would be fine. My mother had no such illusions, having been slapped in the face by life about a million times, starting with her parents' divorce and early death and continuing through my father's untimely departure. She never expected any better. Her intense pessimism was her key to survival. More shit. What a surprise.

How could you do this?

I don't know, Mom, it was normal to us.

How could it be normal to you? Is this how we brought you up? Are you crazy?

Well, look, Mom, I'm better now. I'm over it. They'll get over it too.

Unfortunately, Steve didn't go with Nancy when the van from the rehab came to take her away. He still thought he could quit on his own. He belonged to the carpenter's union in New York, which was full of junkies and alcoholics; compared to the people he worked with, he was an overachiever. He didn't want to take a month off work, didn't want to spend the money for treatment, certainly didn't realize what was going to happen.

We visited Nancy at the rehab center that Christmas; it was a pretty little place, like a prep school campus, not far from Grace and Rod's house in the Poconos. I remember sitting at the Al-Anon meeting she asked me to go to, listening to people tell stories about the nightmare of living with addicted family members, a television set thrown down the stairs, violence and threats and lies. I was so innocent then—so sure that nothing like that would ever happen to me.

Later, at dinner, Nancy introduced us to a new friend named Brian, and I could tell something was going on between them. I wasn't thrilled about it.

When she got home, she told Steve nothing about the new boyfriend, only that she wouldn't live with him anymore unless he stopped getting high. The truth was, she wasn't going to live with him anymore, period. And it wasn't about the new guy. It was that she'd finally made a decision on her own, and she was afraid she wouldn't be able to stick to that one or make any others if she went back with Steve. Her emerging view of things was that I had run the first half of her life and Steve the second and it was time for her to take over.

Steve flew down to Austin thinking once again that he would quit while staying with us, but went into terrible withdrawal and had me calling 800-number help lines, driving him to the emergency room, trying to reach our doctors, doing anything to get some drugs or some relief, but of course nobody gave him either. He was a wreck, his dark eyes frightened, his short curly hair trimmed crookedly, ugly track marks visible on his muscular arms when he took off his hooded sweatshirt. Less than forty-eight hours after he arrived, he was on a plane back north.

Nancy picked him up at the airport and drove him straight to the center, though he made her stop in the city so he could cop. He shot five bags at once, she told me.

Jesus Christ, Nancy, didn't you think he'd OD?

That was nothing, she said. You should have seen me before I checked in in November. I did a big shot in the backseat of the pickup van on the way up there, all scrunched up so they couldn't see me in the rearview mirror, and another in the ladies' room of the place right before they searched me at registration.

By the time Steve came out of rehab, it was all over between him and Nancy. He couldn't believe it. They had been together for thirteen years, since Nancy was seventeen. They had always been a tight, insular couple, and drugs had pushed them even further into their private world. After years of waiting and worrying, he was starting to get HIV symptoms. So now that he was going to die, she was dumping him?

Steve moved into New York City and Nancy stayed out in Jersey. Just as we were getting settled in our new place—three bedrooms and a funky fenced yard for only $700 a month—they had to get rid of the sweet house they'd bought in Bloomfield and put so much work into. She was busy with Narcotics Anonymous, her work as a C.P.A., and the new boyfriend. For all of us, the nineties had begun.

Meanwhile, Steve was calling me all the time, desperate and heartbroken and furious, getting high on and off, and I didn't know what to say to him. I couldn't accept Nancy's decision either. It seemed unfair and sudden and hard-hearted to me too.

I still had no real understanding of addiction, how it destroys everything around it. How heroin becomes number one—no, numbers one through five; everything else you supposedly care about doesn't even start until six. When you are number six, as Nancy and Steve had become to each other, you've got to look out for yourself, because love and honor and trust and even tomorrow morning don't mean a thing to a junkie, even though he will swear up and down that they do. And because he believes it, you believe it too. Until finally one day something so awful happens that you realize it's all bullshit. You haven't even been talking to the person you thought you were talking to.

Nancy saved herself from this, and never did drugs again. Steve, crushed by her abandonment, hearing AIDS jeering at him from the wings, never found his way.

BIRTHDAY PRESENTS

Seven months into my third pregnancy, my company sent me to a computer conference in Nice, France. Tony and Hayes and Sandye came with me, and we went on to Italy when the work part was over. It was my third pregnancy in four years; I was an old hand. Transatlantic flight, big deal; selling software to Europeans on my feet for a week, no problem; treacherous hike on what was hardly more than a goat path along the ocean cliffs of Cinqueterre, pushing Hayes in the stroller—well, this was a little more of a challenge than I'd bargained for. Tony ended up carrying the stroller and almost ended up carrying me, but the stunning views and fragrant tangled terraces of olive trees and grapevines and flowers were worth it.

I ate pasta and zuppa and pizza and gelato and drank a little wine on the side—hey, all the pregnant Italian women were doing it. I even tossed back a grappa with my espresso one morning at 7:30 A.M. at the urging of the ancient regulars at the counter of the shop I'd stopped at during my morning walk. They said it would give my baby a sweet disposition. Hey, I'll try it. After my one obsessively perfect pregnancy had ended in disaster, I gradually relaxed my view of the precautions required. I wasn't going to drink a bottle of vodka, snort some coke, and be responsible for birth defects; I also wasn't going to refuse a morning grappa and think it made any goddamn difference.

The four of us shared a room wherever we went; yes, to save money, but also because it didn't matter. By this time, sex was really over between me and Tony; it wasn't even an issue. At home, we never even thought about trying to get Hayes to sleep in his own room—why bother? The "family bed" theory fit in with the rest of our parenting ideology, but I see now that my support for it was quite provisional. If I'd ever thought I had the chance to participate in anything more interesting than sleeping, I'd have had those kids out of my bedroom in nothing flat.

At the peak of my earth-motherism, I had my second son at home with a midwife, a dear woman named G.B. who ran the mother's support group I went to every week with Hayes, a group devoted to the *Mothering* magazine approach—cotton diapers, homemade baby food, righteous breast-feeding, and herbal remedies. A mother of four herself and a practicing Sikh, G.B. had the boyish figure and waist-length blond hair of a teenager, combined with the gentleness and insight of a tribal elder. You wanted to have a home birth just to hang out with her for twenty-four hours.

My obstetrician, who had shared with me the ordeal of Peewee and the relief of Hayes, was uncomfortable about my having a baby at home, though she agreed to do my prenatal care and to back me up at the hospital if I should need it. In my favor, I had had two vaginal deliveries with no complications (even Peewee was considered a no-complications delivery, believe it or not), and my weekly bouts with the fetal monitor were showing the baby in perfect health.

This doctor and I had been arguing on and off for years anyway. Should I have breast-fed Hayes, given that I might, against all reason, have turned HIV-positive at the last minute and not know it, because it takes a few months to show up on a test? She thought not. I thought so, and wrote long letters to experts around the state to put forth my case and enlist them on my side. If they had disagreed, I would have gotten different experts. I had a lot of conviction about breast-feeding, just as I did about home birth, and it would have taken more than a few doubtful doctors to convince me not to go ahead and do what I wanted to do. I tended to find my own logic irresistible.

Fortunately, Vince did too. He was born at home right on his due date, which was Tony's thirty-third birthday, almost without a hitch. Labor is another one of those things that become dream-like in recollection—like being hit, it is so physical that the memory stays more in your body than your mind, and so painful that as soon as it's over, it starts to seem unreal.

The yellow light of the uncovered bulb in the carport behind our house is my clearest sense memory from that night. We were sitting back there at midnight with G.B. and Nancy, who'd flown down for the event—Hayes was spending the night with a friend—when I decided it was time for Tony's birthday party. My contractions were coming ten minutes apart when I presented him with a CD player with five-disc shuffle; his vinyl holdout days were over. With the assistance of a dance-club dee-jay friend, I had also bought him a bunch of CDs by bands I'd never heard of. Tony's taste in music was very cutting-edge. I knew for sure what he hated—he once removed an Edie Brickell CD from a friend's player and calmly folded it in half, saying, Never do this to fine electronic equipment—but what he would consider cool was way beyond me.

I loved the freedom of not being in the hospital that night. No rules, no paperwork, no bureaucracy, no Big Nurse. The idea that we could have a baby in our very own house, in our very own bed without all that superstructure on top of us was amazing. I could sit outside under the stars, I could walk around naked if the spirit moved me, I could even clean my refrigerator. I felt so powerful, so free. When we got antsy sometime before dawn, we strolled over to the 7-Eleven for a carton of orange juice and a pack of Newports for Tony.

I'm in labor, I told the clerk giddily.

Well, get the hell out of here, she said. Don't you have somewhere you need to be?

Labor progressed relatively slowly until we all got bored, close to noon the next day. G.B. gave me some herbal remedy to speed things up. Soon after, the tea-party phase was over. I threw myself on the bed, hollering like a madwoman. It was two in the afternoon. I guess no one was home in the neighborhood or surely they would have called the police.

Finally, the baby was coming out, all slimy and beautiful, the last and best birthday present for his father. Always good with a scissors, Tony cut the cord himself. Everybody was laughing and crying and I demanded my baby and a glass of champagne.

And that was the birth of Vincent Valdrick Winik, Vincent for Tony's great-uncle who was always called Bill, Valdrick for his grandfather of the squirrel spaghetti sauce.

Vincie La Voo, as he was immediately nicknamed, was a magical child, the baby messiah, we said. Half Jewish, half Catholic, radiantly angelic, born practically in a manger on his father's thirty-third birthday. Hayes was a good and beautiful baby, but this infant was positively charismatic. It must have been that shot of grappa. Even strangers reacted to him with unusual interest. We thought maybe we could put him on cable TV and make some money.

Well, that was a long time ago. He is five now and though still adorable, "messiah" is not the first word that comes to mind.

Tony was more involved in baby care than ever, having left the salon to work at home. I was still at the software company from eight to two, so he took Hayes to his new Montessori school and was with Vincie all morning. I picked Hayes up and took over at two-thirty so Tony could work on clients in the salon he had fixed up at home. Originally described to us by the leasing agent as the "hobby room," Tony's new beauty parlor was a little box off the kitchen with two walls of windows and a door to the backyard. Its tenure as Chez Tony upscaled its appearance considerably.

He painted the walls pink and sponged metallic gold on top, did the trim in deep magenta, and sprayed the ceiling fan gold. He polished the windows and hardwood floors, installed a shampoo sink and hauled in his many chairs: a turquoise fifties hydraulic chair for cutting, a rickety stool for him to perch on, a reclining lounge for shampoos, a massive pink number with a bonnet hair dryer for chemical work, all scavenged from garage sales and thrift shops or lugged over as offerings by clients and friends. He used a weathered wooden Parsons table as a back bar and rolling carts for curlers and cotton and foils. Racks full of dyes and shampoos covered the walls; stacks of back copies of avant-garde British hair magazines were spread on a low table.

The brightly painted walls were decorated with pictures of favorite dead celebrities, postcards of Renaissance virgins, and, framed in ornate gold wood, the label from a bottle of wine we had drunk in Nice, DERRIÈRE LES FAGOTS. We never stopped laughing about that one. Pictures of me and the boys were stuck in the corners of the mirrors; Mexican candles in tall glasses and Day of the Dead figurines fashioned from wood and bits of fabric lined the windowsill: a skeleton dog-walker and his charges, a dentist and patient, a table of cardplayers, and Tony's favorite, a bridal couple. Painted lashes fringed the bride's black eye-pits; a scrap of lace waved from her skull. Beside her, her tuxe-doed, top-hatted groom wore a cadaverous grin, and a tiny bouquet of withered blossoms lay at their feet.

While Tony was cutting hair, he would prop up Vincie's baby carrier in the seat of the hair dryer and hand him his favorite toy, the Red Rings. Two concentric plastic circles with a blue ball in the center, attached by a flexible cable to another ring, this is one of those toys that look absolutely ridiculous to a grown-up, but to a baby is a virtual Rubik's Cube. When the Red Rings didn't keep him quiet, Tony would pick him up and give him the tip of his little finger to suck. In between clients, the two of them would make the rounds—to the coffee roasters, the plant nursery, the beauty supply, the doctor. For years, Tony rarely visited his doctor without at least one small child in tow.

Dr. Ray Benito was a very important person in Tony's life. A young, intelligent, thoughtful, and overworked man, Benito cared for dozens of HIV and AIDS patients, for whom his genuine sympathy made him far more than a doctor: he was a confessor, a counselor, a cheerleader, a seer, a hand-holder. When Tony first became his patient in 1986, Benito confirmed that the night sweats, swollen glands, and diarrhea he occasionally suffered from were symptoms of ARC—AIDS-related-complex. At that time, there was no accepted treatment or medication for patients in the early phases of the disease.

Right after Peewee died, Tony and I had become interested in macrobiotics; for about four years we were tofu-heads, eating brown rice and kale and pink-radish pickles all the time. Hanging around the East-West Center, we met other people with HIV who were trying to improve their condition through diet, alternative treatment, and "attitudinal healing." Though he genuinely liked the food and was treated by an acupuncturist for several years to boost his immune system, Tony's attitude was never in danger of getting healed. He loved to dish the New Age scene—they may have found themselves, he said, but they've pretty much lost everybody else. When he learned that Michio Kushi, the head macro up in Boston, was a big cigarette smoker, he was delighted.

Benito thought alternative approaches were fine, and wrote

letters supporting my attempt to get the insurance company to pay for the acupuncture treatments. That never worked, but they did pay their portion of Benito's bills and the various medications Tony took starting in 1989, many of them outrageously expensive. One of the reasons I never left my job at the software company was that we needed the insurance. Once diagnosed with HIV, Tony never would have been able to get another policy.

By the time Vincie was born, Tony was on AZT. His T-cell count was about 400, as it had been since Benito first measured. (A normal T-cell count is well over 1,000; below 400 is grounds for an AIDS diagnosis.) Benito monitored his condition every three months, less frequently if everything was fine, more often if something came up. Tony had continual congestion in his lungs that occasionally flared up into bronchitis; on a few occasions, Benito diagnosed a mild case of pneumocystis pneumonia (PCP), but these rarely caused Tony to spend even a day in bed.

If I could get the time off from work, I would join Tony's entourage on the visits to the doctor—when there was a crisis or a treatment decision to make, of course, but more often I just wanted to see Ray. He had the classic messy hair and rumpled clothes of the busy young doctor who has no time to take care of himself, but behind his wire-rimmed glasses, his blue eyes were as calm and kind as a kindergarten teacher's. I loved to feel his soothing presence, to hear his thorough explanations, his jokes, his words of encouragement. I thought maybe the sight of our happy little family, the chalk drawings the kids left on his blackboard, brightened his trauma- and tragedy-filled days, too.

MY MOTHER-IN-LAW

I woke before sunrise to Tony leaning over me, his hair brushing my cheek, his voice in my ear. Now or never, he said. Do you still want to go?

Next to me, baby Vincie's eyes popped open as well. He gazed sleepily at his father, who automatically reached to investigate his diaper. As I attempted to clamber out of bed without waking the other of our offspring, I stumbled over a blanketed heap on the floor and froze, checking to see whom I might have disturbed. For a moment, it looked like all was clear. I quietly began to dress as Tony finished changing Vincie's diaper and rolled him back onto his stomach, rhythmically patting his back in the snooze-producing fashion of which he was a master.

Was it the rustle of a T-shirt, the scrape of a zipper, the tiny squish of a contact lens poked into a half-open eye? Within minutes, all five of our roommates were awake.

Are you going bike-riding? asked little Louie plaintively. Can we come? Aged nine, ten, and twelve, he and his brothers were our new nephews. But with their identical blond crew cuts and minimal variation in size, they were as yet indistinguishable to my unpracticed eye. What's more, they all had names beginning with the same letter. In desperation, I had begun to refer to them as Huey, Dewey and Louie.

Oh, please, Aunt Marion.

So much for the romantic sunrise bike ride. We figured we'd take the kids and let the other grown-ups sleep. But despite our frantic shushing, the toilette of boys and babies followed by a group exodus through the living room awakened Tony's brother Frankie and his new wife Debbie, mother of the duck brothers, sleeping on the fold-out couch. Frankie's moans were the last straw for young Uncle Sam, snatching him from whatever Mars-to-Earth broadcast he picked up on the headphones he slept with and dragging him disbelieving from his blankets on the floor. Ah, the righteous bitching of the childless, who believe they have a right to sleep in the morning. My in-laws, behind the closed door of the other bedroom, dozed firmly through the entire ordeal, or pretended to.

Eventually, the lot of us ended up out at the bike rack in the dark, unlocking our rented cruisers. Dewey and Louie had forgotten their combination, causing Huey to pummel them then run back to the apartment to get it for them. Tony and I exchanged glances, watching the love-hate yin-yang of brotherhood with tender horror, knowing it lurked just around the corner of our lives. Meanwhile, baby Vince nestled in the front-pack against my chest, snoozing again, and Hayes was enthroned and helmeted in a child's seat on the back of Tony's bike. We go beach, he announced. We see sun.

The beach was wide and flat and silent, the tide gleaming close to our tires as we pedaled along the tight-packed sand at the ocean's edge. The three boys took the lead, Tony and I followed with our small passengers, and Frank and Debbie trailed behind, snatching romantic moments wherever possible. Getting married with three kids already in the equation gave them what is a still unfinished case of newlyweditis.

Uncle Sam came zooming up from behind, shirtless and Ray-Banned and wearing fluorescent swim trunks. Slowpokes! he jeered, passing us, and disappeared into the distance with his fan club—Huey et al.—hot on his heels. Later they would return talking all at once about some crab corpse they had discovered, then produce the wretched specimen itself from a bicycle basket.

The baby in the front-pack opened his round blue eyes and looked up. He seemed amazed. His mother's face in a moving sky, the cry of a gull, the sensation of movement, the salty wind ruffling his single tuft of hair—who knows what amazed him? Ahead of us, the sun was a flaming peach, unrolling a golden carpet over the water. I had the feeling I could ride straight across.

That vacation in September of 1990 was our third trip to Hilton Head Island, a destination that neither Tony nor I probably ever would have chosen to visit on our own, but which had become a regular fixture in our lives since Grace and Rod bought a time-share at a Marriott resort. This weeklong sojourn every year just after Labor Day had assumed a fixed position as one of his parents' annual splurges. They did not live a luxurious life, but there were certain things they liked to do; Grace was adept at saving money and nursing her credit line during the off months to do these in relatively high style. These things invariably fell into one or both of two categories: "for the kids!" or "vacation!" Christmas and Disney World were so highly qualified on both counts that they were independent subgenres.

Christmas, of course, is a major event for all Catholics, but Grace's interpretation of the importance of the holiday veered somewhat from the traditional view. Her Christmas, for example, gave no outward signs of being a religious holiday. It was a shopping spree of ungodly proportions undertaken in a spirit of righteousness and abandon, with secondary emphases on the trimming of trees and the preparation and eating of meals. Hayes, celebrating his first Christmas at the age of seven months, had received well over a dozen presents from her, not including Christmassy bric-a-bric like tree ornaments, Russian Santa Claus dolls, and reindeer snow-domes. I'm not complaining. I myself scored big from the J. Crew catalog. This obsessive giving of presents was no standard submission to commercialism; it was a rite of financial sacrifice with a big payoff in joy.

If Christmas was the major holiday of Grace's "for the kids!" religion, Disney World was its Mecca. Shangri-La, Eden, El Dorado, New Atlantis: I don't know why my thesaurus does not list the Magic Kingdom in this group. If she wasn't taking her own grandchildren down there, she would move onto grandnieces and -nephews and neighbors. While another woman might have been somewhat perturbed at her son's marriage to a woman with half-grown children, Grace thought Frankie's action not only normal but commendable and propitious. It was, in fact, what Rod had done when he married her.

For Grace, the whole purpose of money is to spend it on children, and Disney World is the ultimate place to do it. In fact, it is in her adoration of Disney World that one sees the dizzy kid in this otherwise brusquely maternal woman, running around in a Donald Duck sun visor and Day-Glo plastic sunglasses, her stout torso encased in a Minnie T-shirt. She loves the rides, the theme hotels, the restaurants, the souvenirs, the monorails and buses, the furry characters giving autographs, the pats of butter cleverly shaped like Mickey Mouse. She has been there so many times, seeing the 360-degree film about China has got to have the familiar quality of a mass.

Grace's prodigious generosity toward children big and small, her enthusiasm for vacations, and her cavalier attitude about sleeping arrangements combine to create in my mother-in-law an alarming propensity for cramming a very large number of people into a very small space. This became increasingly problematic at Hilton Head, where the two-bedroom condo did not expand as did the guest list, on an annual basis. The first year, right after they bought the time-share, it was just us and them, me pregnant with Peewee. She refers to this as "the time you had those purple things hanging out of your hair."

Despite our distaste for the security gates, highly obvious building codes, and general Big Brother Is Making Sure You Have a Great Vacation atmosphere of Hilton Head's planned resort community—Tony speculated that the Spanish moss was hung from the trees by a crew of decorators—we managed to have quite a nice time.

The resort was Disney World–esque in its manicured loveliness. From the melon-carpeted apartment to the pristine beach, a private boardwalk wound through towering trees and banks of flowers, past three hot tubs, two swimming pools, and a tropical-snack hut. Just outside the door, there was an old-fashioned wooden swing by a pond complete with blooming waterlilies and friendly butterflies. Out front, there were bike rentals; we spent hours each day cruising the flat, shady trails inland or the packed sand at the water's edge. We lay on the wide beach in the early autumn sun, me reading *Our Gang* and Tony with his perennial Anne Rice—this is one of the ways I knew he couldn't die, because Anne Rice would continue writing books and it was not possible that he wouldn't be there to read them—and we ate out every night, which would have been great, except for the less than thrilling restaurants on Hilton Head and one other little thing.

When two people as bossy as both Grace and me spend any length of time in each other's company, conflict invariably ensues. Since each is accustomed to making all the plans and decisions—where and what time to eat dinner, who to include, whether to dress, how many cars to take to the restaurant, and what route to follow—snits can hardly be avoided. Nothing, and I mean *nothing,* is too trivial for a contretemps between control freaks.

The first few years, I struggled to express my views on dining (What about the clam place? Maybe we should just stay home and order a pizza?), until finally I realized it was a lost cause. I was in the presence of a power greater than my own. Still, what killed me was the way she made the decision, without even acknowledging she was making it. It was always Rod. "We'll see what Rod feels like." These consultations with Rod, who was virtually cipherlike in his taciturnity, were carried on in secret, if indeed they were carried on at all. Any suggestion one might make would be met with a little nod and "I think Rod may be in the mood for Japanese."

The correct and only response is: Yum. Japanese. Unless it turns out Rod wants steaks. Yum. Steaks.

Our second trip to Hilton Head—"the time you had that platinum-blond crew cut"—was more crowded than the first, as Tony's half-brother Sam joined us, along with Aunt Jo and her husband and a couple of their grandchildren. This time, our third year, my hairstyle was almost normal, but the guest list had swelled to thirteen. And there were still only two bedrooms in the condominium.

Nonetheless, I was in a fairly jolly mood that trip, high on my nursing hormones and having given up all pretense of decision-making. There remained, however, at least one sore spot between Grace and me, one which was never discussed because Grace does not believe in discussing things. This obstacle to our interpersonal coziness had surfaced at our first meeting, seven years earlier, when I'd brought up the long-unspoken fact of Tony's gayness. Where it was my family's habit to turn any bad news into a joke, or at least a commonplace, as quickly as possible, in Grace and Tony's world, skeletons stayed in their closets. It was unbelievable to me, though typical of them, that Tony still had not told her about his HIV status.

I always want to talk about everything, especially bad things, usually over and over until all points of view are understood by everyone and repeated exposure to air has rendered the poison harmless. To me, not talking about a problem makes it far worse than it is. To Grace, talking about it is the worst thing you can do, drawing attention to it and blowing it out of proportion. If you don't talk about it, you can just pretend it's not there. In fact, the person who talks about the bad thing is usually considered to have done a worse thing than whoever did the bad thing in the first place.

A key corollary: None of her sons ever do anything bad.

One afternoon, Tony came up to me on the beach, where I was camped out with my book and the baby under a makeshift tent of towels. He had been building sand castles with the boys down by the water. We're out of suntan lotion, Mar, he said. I'm going to the drugstore.

Bummer, I said, wishing we had bought the suntan lotion before we left home. The island was like an airport as far as prices were concerned—they knew they had you. If I'd realized we needed suntan lotion, I could have at least picked some up that morning at the grocery store. Now Tony would be loose in a foofy Hilton Head boutique drugstore with the credit card; we would probably end up with at least five tubes of various European gelées and après-soleils in a spectrum of SPF's. Tony was his mother's son in two ways. He loved to shop, and he perceived himself as someone who should have everything he wanted.

I had more or less indulged him on both these counts in the years we'd been together, but as we'd come to have more disposable income, the differential in the rapidity with which we intended to dispose of it had become obvious. I was good for the occasional splurge, vacations, fancy dinners out, extravagant birthday gifts. If I let him, Tony's splurges would have been daily.

CDs, clothes, biscotti, exotic skin cleansers, hardcover best-sellers—does one ever really have enough of these? Should any-one really visit New York without acquiring a new pair of shoes? And because the vast majority of our money had been earned by me and because we now had two children, a mortgage, a car payment, etc., my sugar-mamaism had begun to give way to a certain stinginess, which Tony at this point more or less ac-cepted, rushing to the movie store to return the soon-to-be-overdue videos before midnight without a peep, or accepting my cautionary statements about not spending a fortune on sun lo-tion with obedient reassurances.

His mother, however, upon overhearing our initial exchange about the lotion, and the later one, when he returned and I asked how much he had spent, became quite miffed, though it took me a while to figure out the cause of her suddenly colder treatment.

It was fourteen dollars and sixty-three cents?

It was the cheapest one they had, Mar.

The cheapest one was fourteen sixty-three?

I got a magazine and a pack of cigarettes too.

A pack of cigarettes? I thought you had a carton.

It's smoked.

Oh.

This $14.63 was symbolic to everyone. To Grace, it was a symbol of my not treating her son right. To me, it was a symbol of the way in which I tried frantically to retain control over our money, $14.63 at a time. To Tony, it was a symbol of the fact that it wasn't really *our* money at all.

Our financial relationship was already that of a parent to a child. And I was not as indulgent a parent as Grace. I had been once, but I had changed.

Why is your mother mad at me? I whispered to Tony the next

day. She's definitely giving me the pressed lips and the short answers.

She's not mad at you.

She is too. I think it's about the suntan lotion.

What about the suntan lotion?

When I gave you a hard time for spending too much money.

Oh, for God's sake, Marion, don't worry about it. It's none
of her business.

But I did worry about it. And since I couldn't bring it up directly—against the rules!—I launched into some big speech that
afternoon about how we still couldn't sell the old condo and the
rent was much less than the payment, how the plumbing in the
house had had to be redone, how Tony didn't have much time to
take clients with the baby in the house all the time, etc., etc.,
hoping to justify my behavior to her. I don't know whether this
sob story made much of an impression, but she did give me an
indication our last night at Hilton Head that forgiveness was
more or less mine. It was subtle, it was indirect, and it was far
from gushy, but in dealing with Grace I had become a veritable
semiotician of the minuscule.

One of the virtues of an island that's only five miles wide is
that twelve hours after you've watched the sun climb up over
the ocean on one side, you can head over to the other and do
cocktails at sunset. Unless you've got kids to entertain, babies to
feed, thirteen people's whims to harmonize, and your mother-
in-law telling you what to do all the time, then you may never
set foot in a bar at all. By our last day, I was feeling a little down-
trodden about this. But as the afternoon drew to a close, our
kids were napping and we were stuck in the condo minding
them, flipping through back issues of *What's Doing on Hilton Head
This Week* and *The Happy Islander.*

Then Grace slid open the glass doors from the deck, threw

Tony the car keys, lifted the baby from my arms, and plopped herself down on the couch. It's almost five-thirty, you two, she scolded. Better hurry. Though she sounded as if she were sending us to finish our chores rather than liberating us from them, I believe the small creases around the corners of her mouth may have been a smile.

We made it to the bar in time to claim a table on the deck and a pair of daiquiris while the sky was still turning colors. A just-married couple at a neighboring table endeared themselves to us by asking if we were on our honeymoon too. It was a revelation to imagine we still looked young and romantic to someone. We took sunset pictures of them with their camera, they returned the favor, and soon it was dusk and we were tilting back in our wooden rockers, the second round of cocktails under way.

In my daiquiri haze, I believed this was forever, believed I'd be there every September for the rest of my life. I could just see my photo albums, the pictures of the kids at ever-increasing ages in the wooden swing outside the Marriott, Tony and I with gray hair and cardigan sweaters on rented bicycles. By the turn of the century, I imagined, there would be twenty-five of us in the condo. They'd have named a dish at the Sukiyaki House after me.

KODAK MOMENT

I've dumped four years' worth of snapshots out of a box onto the kitchen table; they've been sitting there for a week. I made beautiful photo albums from the day Tony and I met until Vince was born, right up through that last year at Hilton Head, but by early 1991 the pictures were accumulating so fast and there was so much else going on, I just threw them into a box. Last year, Tony hauled it out and was going to make albums for my Christmas present, but he never finished. By then, I'd stopped taking pictures. I couldn't stand to add to the mess. I could no longer figure out what I wanted to remember.

Nineteen ninety-one through 1994, on the table, jumbled together: babies in bluebonnets, little boys in bluebonnets, a black cat and a Ninja turtle going trick-or-treating with their father, the ghost. Tony's hair grown long, cut short, pulled back, Tony doing a friend's hair for her wedding. Us kissing on a boat at sunset, kissing at somebody's ranch, kissing at a pizza place in Brooklyn.

Here's the backyard with the pool, the backyard without the pool, the backyard torn up for pool construction and Vince in a diaper, playing in the rubble, I can almost hear the mariachi music from the workers' radio. I remember I imagined that music would be sealed inside the pool forever, a pool with a Mexican heart. Here we are at the Space Needle in Seattle, Hayes took this one, and these too—Tony hiking the great gray desolation of Mount St. Helens with baby Vince on his back.

A rare shot of Tony on skates, showing off for Hayes and his friends. We're at the ice rink at the shopping mall, bright-colored flags hanging from the ceiling, four-year-old boys lean-ing over the rail transfixed, Tony a spinning blur at center ice, his arms crossed over his chest. At Hayes's urging, he tried a few jumps, amazing not just his son but other spectators and even himself with the height and speed of those long-unpracticed moves. Will you show me how to do that, Daddy? Hayes begged. As soon as you're old enough, Tony promised him.

Here we all are up at Pete and Shelley's place, our first visit since the summer Peewee died. This trip, Sandye came along with her niece, Lindsay, and took a zillion pictures: Hayes and Lindsay on a nature walk with Shelley, Vincie caught giggling in the outhouse, silly grown-ups drinking beer and sitting in each other's laps, Tony and Pete skimming rocks across the creek.

Here's New Orleans and more New Orleans, an endless pa-rade of New Orleans—graveyards, alligators, carnival floats, people in costume, kids on shoulders reaching to catch beads. What in God's name is this? An upside-down topless dancer doing a walkover into Tony's lap?

I search for something to sort the photographs into, but the only type of container I seem to have enough of is loaf pans. For a person who does not bake, I have a surprising number of them. I do my sorting with the trash can close at hand, as my mother taught me. Be ruthless; all but the best have to go. The first time I saw her going through an envelope of photos and winging half of them into the garbage I was shocked. Now I understand. Edit-ing is essential. The accidental double chin, the red-lit eyes, the out-of-focus smile: out. Even the apparent meaninglessness of those photographic mistakes suggests what you don't intend to record.

What a blur these years are to me. Too recent to have re-duced themselves to the relevant detail, as have the Year We Met, the Year We Got Married, the Year Peewee Died. Which one was the Year Things Started to Go Wrong? Because when my life was in ruins around me, I should not have been as surprised as I was. There must have been warnings, but if I saw them, I averted my eyes. The shutter did not snap. This is what I had to do; there were stories I had to tell myself, had to believe, to make myself go on, to hold everything together. The story of the Bright Side, the Silver Lining, the happy fiction of the photographs, the one I was knitting together in the act of taking them. The holidays, the birthdays, the smiling children, the affectionate couple, the rhythm of the seasons, home improvements, the Hollywood montage of how well things are going, how sweet they are together.

There is no picture, for example, of this: Throughout the early months of 1991, when Vincie was still a tiny baby, the ATM withdrawals listed on our bank statement were getting higher and higher. The first month, I didn't really notice it. The second month, I thought maybe I'd forgotten to write something down. The third month, I called the bank. It turned out you could tell which of our two cards had been used to make the withdrawal by a code number, and all the mysterious withdrawals, the $100s, the $150s, were on Tony's card. By the time I understood what was going on, he had spent over $1,500.

It took ironclad, incontrovertible proof to get him to stop playing dumb. Later, even proof didn't work. Tony became a master of the *Gaslight* effect, as in that old movie where Ingrid Bergman's husband tries to drive her crazy by dimming and turning up the gas-lit sconces in their house, then claiming that she's just imagining it.

I found him sitting on the back steps the day I got the bank statement, out on what we called "the pink patio" because after the pool was finished he had painted the cement and the poles of the old carport in silly carousel colors, pink and blue. That cold, rainy March, it was the only bright spot in the whole muddy backyard.

I thrust the papers from the bank toward him. Look at this, Tony.

He wouldn't take them out of my hand, didn't want to look at the markings I had made with a yellow highlighter pen.

I bought coke, he said finally. There was a horrible clatter of breaking glass as the city recycling truck made its stop at our house.

Coke? What the hell for? How could you do this? I cried. Who knows except me? When were you doing it? Where? Did you get dope too, Tony? Did you drive the kids around high?

He was hunched over, smoking, frustrated at having to answer and in so much guilty pain. Then he stubbed out the cigarette.

No, he sighed, not with the kids. You just don't understand how it is, Marion. You don't know what it's like to be dying. You don't know how I feel.

Oh, for Christ's sake. You're not fucking dying, Tony. Not yet, anyway.

I never believed this was a good enough excuse. It *wasn't* a good enough excuse. I knew that once he believed he was dying, he would be. He would stop eating brown rice and miso soup and getting acupuncture treatments. He would never read the Bernie Siegel books I kept trying to force on him. Instead of waiting for doom to surprise him, he would throw himself into the grip of a doom he thought he could control. Or the converse: a bliss he could turn on and off at will. A white noise louder than all the voices in his head.

Tony would rather give up than lose, would rather surrender his happiness than have it torn from him, would rather anes-

thetize himself than deal with pain. He was not a person of spiritual faith, not an angel or a martyr. If he couldn't escape, he
would rush wildly into the dark. By outending the end, he
would be in control.

Perhaps because I never really believed he was dying, I
couldn't accept that he did and therefore couldn't empathize. I
could understand intellectually how he felt, but I couldn't feel
it. This was both a shortcoming and a gift, because though I see
now that I failed him in sympathy and ultimately failed him in
love, I did not fail him in strength. I did not give up on him until
long after he had given up on himself. As I am not the first to
note, what is now called denial used to be known as hope.

But at that moment I was nothing but angry. As far as I was
concerned, this whole ATM incident had nothing to do with
AIDS and everything to do with money and trust. There I was,
freaking out about a $14.63 bottle of suntan lotion or a pile
of CDs, minuscule extravagances compared to this robbery,
this violation. He had stolen that money from me and from the
kids, had concealed it and lied about it until the last possible
minute.

At one time, money had been a symbol of love in our relationship. From here on out, it was an instrument of punishment.

I took away his ATM card and his credit card, though I left his
name on our bank account and let him keep his checkbook,
since he still had to go grocery shopping and buy gas for his car. I
watched the bank statements like a hawk, at least for a while.

Perhaps it seems strange that I was so shocked by this discov-
ery about Tony and the coke. After all, from the day we met,
Tony and I did drugs. Drugs were a cornerstone of our social
life, our relationship, even of who we were as individuals. But I
thought those days were over. And even if they weren't, Tony in
the laundry room doing a whole gram by himself in the middle

of the day was not about social life, was not about our relationship, was not about anything I could understand.

Among all my other reactions, there was a little unexpected
resentment: how could he do all that coke and not even offer me
any? Now why was I thinking that if I was so reformed, so pure?
My resistance to drugs was very provisional; the provision was
that they not be in front of my face. Put a baby in my arms and
get the shit out of the house and I do all right. Otherwise, I was
not such a saint, as would become clear over the next few years.

After this incident, I went back to my happy story—what
else could I do? Drugs disappeared from the picture, or at least
went underground, again. We worked and played and went on
trips, celebrated birthdays, entertained houseguests, gave our
annual Oscar party, went out to dinner and movies and night-
clubs and watched *L.A. Law* with Scott and Lexanne every Thursday night. Just like in the pictures.

EARTHQUAKE

By the end of the summer of 1992, it had become much harder to pretend everything was going to be fine. Like an earthquake, the shift in our landscape began with a series of rumbles and tremors, then a shocking jolt—like so many shocking jolts these days, it arrived in the form of a message on my answering machine—and finally a series of subjolts and quivers as damage spread along all the fault lines of our marriage. After that summer, the ground beneath us was never solid again. The buildings began to crumble; the structural damage was never repaired.

Over the preceding year and a half—since the ATM incident—the oscillation between Pollyanna World and Life in Hell had become more jarring and pronounced. Among our closest friends, three marriages were in various stages of falling apart, and Steven had gotten much sicker. He had been hospitalized several times, was losing his vision, had stopped working. Tony and he could hardly stand to talk anymore, they depressed each other so much. I had been up there one weekend to visit him, and spent most of the time arguing about Nancy, the rest fantasizing about his good-looking roommate while Steven napped.

By this time, my sexual deprivation was one of the primary facts of my existence. I literally could not remember the last time Tony and I had made love, and now that pregnancy and nursing were over, I thought about sex all the time. I checked out guys as a single woman would. I considered calling a phone sex number from the personals. Even in the essays I wrote for our local alternative newspaper, the *Austin Chronicle,* I audibly throbbed. My friends were sympathetic: Yes, of course you're going crazy. Go right ahead, have an affair!

Our last Mardi Gras, in the spring of 1992, was a strange combination of fun with the kids and adults-only Saturnalia. Lowell and Sue, who had become our permanent New Orleans hosts since Shelley and Pete moved to the boondocks, had two kids as well, a six-year-old daughter and a little boy Vince's age. We spent our days and early evenings doing Kiddie Gras: day parades, the neighborhood playground, the strangely endearing white alligator at the aquarium, a ride on a paddle-wheel riverboat. Hayes, nearly four, was a seasoned paradegoer. He knew which beads to angle for and which cars threw bubble gum. He was collecting doubloons for show-and-tell at his Montessori school. Vince, at one and a half, could still be carried, and often had to be, to prevent him from toddling off into the sunset.

Tony was the most natural and willing parent among us, the one who got up early to change diapers and pour cereal while everyone slept off their hangovers, the one who kept the gang of kids together at the parades, the one who would ferry them home on his shoulders if they were tired. Everybody loves their own children, but, just like his mother, Tony loved kids in general and never resented either the time or the slave labor they required.

After the members of the junior set were all bathed and in their PJs and snug in their beds, their baby-sitter ensconced in front of the television, we tried to have as much fun as humanly possible in the hours left until morning. This usually involved consuming vast quantities of alcohol and whatever drugs anyone could come up with, going from bar to bar in the French Quarter half the night. Unfortunately, neither we nor any of the other couples we were hanging out with were getting along very well, and the level of intoxication we aspired to was often no help.

On Fat Tuesday itself, Tony and I went our separate ways, he in a Day of the Dead skeleton getup and I in a painted velvet number from the market in Nuevo Laredo. He met a bunch of people from Birmingham, a B-52's-ish band and their hangers-on. One of this group, a pale, skinny architect named Tomé, kept turning up everywhere we went; he seemed to be Tony's new best friend. Late that night, one of the other women and I, both too drunk to stand up any longer, went home before everyone else and more or less had sex in the taxi, to the delight of the driver, then continued after he dropped us off, on our friends' front lawn. Not a word was said the next day, but I'm sure people wondered what our lingerie was doing out in the street.

That June, Tony and I drove down to Mexico with the kids. We had been talking for years about living in Mexico, and it seemed like the moment might be coming. Hayes would start kindergarten in the fall of 1993, so we really had only one year left. I thought I could take an unpaid leave from work, maybe apply for a writing fellowship, and spend the time down there working. By this time, I was recording some of the essays I'd published in the Chronicle for National Public Radio and had a few national magazines I wrote for regularly, though it was no small feat to find time for these activities in my working-mom schedule. Perhaps in Mexico I could get my old great-writer plan back on track.

We had met a woman who had a house in the mountains outside Guanajuato, and she told us to go down and look at it, see if we thought it was in good enough shape to live there for a while. We fell in love with the city and the house, and began to talk as if we were actually going to do it. I would write, Tony would watch the kids, we'd have the three-dollar plate lunch at one of the little cafés near the university every day at noon. We'd be best friends with all the expats, we'd watch American movies on the VCR in the pizza restaurant, the oldest children of the large, beautiful Mormon family in the hobbit house in the hills would be our baby-sitters.

Right after we got home from that trip, Sue, our Mardi Gras hostess, invited Tony to spend a week with her at a spa in Florida; she thought it would be good for his health. During our last visit, she'd noticed the change in his condition. His headaches had become severe and frequent, and he had thrush in his mouth. In May, Benito had diagnosed him with full-blown AIDS, based on his T-cell count, which had dropped to 150 despite the AZT. Since AZT wasn't helping, Benito had switched him to a different antiviral, DDI, and added an antifungal for the thrush. For the headaches, he prescribed a decongestant, a muscle relaxer, and an ever-increasing quantity of Tylenol 4, a codeine-heavy pain reliever.

The spa sounded like a good idea, but since the embezzlement of the preceding year, I had officially retired as sugar mama. Doctor bills, yes; spa, no. Tony's luxuries were limited to those he could afford on his income from hairdressing, which didn't cover much more than cigarettes and CDs, gas for his car, his part of the check at a restaurant. Sue, who wasn't making a fortune from her civil rights law practice but had recently become involved with an obstetrician friend in a profitable business renting hormone pumps to fend off premature labor, offered to pick up the tab for the trip. So off he went.

That week at the spa was one of the longest periods we'd ever been separated from each other, and the first time we'd been apart since the kids were born. At the time, it was a big scary deal to me to be a single mom for a week. Managing the house and yard and kids and the laundry without Tony's help was a serious challenge; he did so much. In his absence, everything from the morning plant-watering to the ritual late-night wiping of the counters was up to me. But I managed more easily than I would have expected.

Tony had a great time that week, the only guy in the place and everyone's darling. He quit smoking, he did water aerobics, he roller-bladed down the boardwalk every day. He ate platefuls of raw fruits and vegetables, along with the baked potatoes and buttered noodles the spa chef served her skinny boy at every meal right under the dieting ladies' covetous noses. One night after dinner, he put auburn lowlights in Sue's blond hair and then everybody else wanted their hair done too.

Despite all this, my incorrigible bon vivant managed to come home in less than mint condition, having escaped the last night and met up with old friends in Fort Lauderdale, barely remembering to stop partying in time to catch his plane. But once the hangover wore off, I could see the spa had been a good influence. He stayed off cigarettes, and every morning before dawn would get up and take an hour-long walk, then come home and eat half a watermelon. If my mother or somebody was around to watch the kids, I would go with him. He took the same route we used to drive to make the kids fall asleep in their car seats when they refused to go down for their naps, and he was fast. From my vantage point a few steps behind, I could see the athlete in him, the boy who used to get up at five every morning to work on his double axel.

Tony's thirty-fifth and Vincie's second birthday were that July; Tony's parents were in town. We had a kid party for Vince during the day, then Tony and I left for the Four Seasons hotel, where I had booked a room. We sat by the pool drinking champagne, then met some friends at a French restaurant for dinner. Afterward, they came back to the room for more drinks and a little cocaine. It was the usual talktalktalktalktalk, everyone psychoanalyzing each other at once, until finally we ran out of drugs, booze, Polaroid film, and cigarettes, and they all disappeared.

Did we make love that night? I doubt it. I don't think we did the year before either, the year I surprised him with an overnight trip to New Orleans. I suppose I was trying to set a sexual scenario by getting us these hotel rooms, but sex was never the main event once we got there, and usually was not on the agenda at all. I would no longer put myself on the line with a big seduction, so instead of my being explicitly rejected, it was more as if we had just forgotten about it.

What I will never forget about being in bed at the Four Seasons that night is the strange conversation we had about Sean Spencer, a young computer programmer at my office.

We had run into Sean at a restaurant a few days earlier while out to dinner with Tony's parents and the boys. I'd stopped by his table to say hi to him and another guy I knew. Sean was wearing a white cotton shirt with the sleeves rolled up, and his forearms were dark tan against it. His hair was dark and curly, his lips, wide and generous, his eyes, melted chocolate. His features were so perfect they were almost pretty, but his height and his mustache and the way he dressed—twenty-something grunge, flannel shirts and ripped jeans—were pure boy. He *was* a boy, just a kid to us older women around the office, a kid from Wyoming who was barely twenty when he came to the company, and was still finishing college. I mean, we appreciated his potential, but he was a child. What's more, he had shaved his head the summer before and looked really weird for months.

By now, he was twenty-three, his hair had grown back, and he wasn't such a kid to me anymore.

That Sean Spencer is the cutest guy in Austin, I announced when I returned to the table. How much more innocent could I have been, making that comment to my husband and his parents? I was completely shocked a few nights later in the bed at the Four Seasons when Tony asked me, out of the blue, if I ever thought about fucking Sean Spencer.

What? I said. What are you talking about? What makes you ask that?

I just wondered. You're always saying how he's so cute and everything.

That he is, I said, wondering what the hell Tony was getting at. Well . . . I guess I wouldn't mind.

I propped myself up on my elbow and looked into his face. What about you? Would you want to fuck him?

Actually, said Tony, if you two did it, I'd like to watch.

I knew that he and Juan had had experiences like this, but as far as I knew, they had been awful. Was this his way of saying he was attracted to Sean too? Would seeing me with someone else make him want me more? We had slept with a third person once, ages ago when we first moved to Austin. It was our coke dealer, a very good-looking heterosexual man. Though it had been a pleasant experience, it had never happened again, and in any case, this time I could tell that Tony was not really suggesting a threesome.

I don't think I ever knew exactly what Tony liked sexually; as far as I could see, he liked the same things as other men I'd been with, but a lot less often. From my point of view, it seemed that he was just not a very sexual person. For though I never had any ongoing feeling that he wanted me, he gave no sign of being attracted to other people, either. Though gayness was still a part of his identity, his involvement in gay life and his gay sexuality seemed to consist mainly of reading mainstream novels and memoirs by gay men—*The Swimming Pool Library,* for example, or something by Paul Monette. Yet he seemed to have no urge to bring the sex scenes he enjoyed reading about to life off the page. I don't know if he repressed that part of himself because of our marriage, or if it just wasn't there. But one thing I was to learn for certain—if sex wasn't all that important to him, fidelity was critical.

However, aside from the less decipherable implications of his asking about Sean Spencer, which I have not to this day fully unraveled, the conversation at the hotel that night seemed to support my impression that it was okay for me to have an affair. In any event, by the next morning I was obsessed with the idea of fucking Sean.

I xeroxed a poem about kissing from my first book and left it in his chair at work. The rest of the week we were going down to the parking garage to smoke cigarettes together, sending provocative E-mail messages back and forth, making jokes about sexual harassment. That Friday, we made a date to have a drink after work. His girlfriend was out of town.

I told Tony that I had to go over to the hospital that evening to visit a young woman with cerebral palsy. That's the kind of excuse you need when you're about to commit adultery. You're not out messing around, you're, um, volunteering at the hospital. Going to services at the synagogue. Raising money for the Red Cross. You want to go for all the virtue you can get.

But my volunteer work would have to wait. I was a long-dormant volcano, scheduled to erupt that Friday night. I picked up Sean at seven and drove to the Midway Club, a dark, seedy bar full of leathery old bubbas where we figured we weren't likely to run into anyone we knew. Within thirty minutes of our arrival, I was sitting on Sean's lap, facing him, kissing him with total abandon, smashed on the shots of tequila and beer I'd been pouring down my throat. He was somewhat nervous at first, but when halfhearted protests failed to discourage me, he gave up and kissed me back with equal passion, running his fingers over the bare skin under my loose white shirt.

Apparently recognizing that public decency did not figure in our concerns at that moment, the bartender came over and asked us to leave. We made it no further than the parking lot, me half-lying across the hood of someone's car, then wedged into the front seat of my own. Even without his incredible beauty, I would have been lost, massively overdosed on adrenaline and hormones and lust. It had been so long, I had almost forgotten.

Being with Sean that night opened a Pandora's box of re-pressed sexual energy, one that had been shut for almost ten years. I could not manage to get it closed again. Sexual energy tore through my being like rainwater after a drought. It trans-formed me, possessed me. I became someone a little different than I had ever been before.

After the night at the Midway Club, things heated up out of control. Trying to slow things down, or perhaps move them to a different track, Sean suggested I have a pool party at my house and invite him and his girlfriend as well as some other people from the office. Actually, he and Tony already knew each other; Tony had cut his hair a couple of times, and I think they'd even gone roller-blading together.

Contrary to Sean's intentions, the party did not slow things down, only compounded our sins by putting our partners in a position where they were unwittingly friendly to the person re-sponsible for their betrayal. I had a long conversation with Sean's cute twenty-one-year-old girlfriend with her big blue eyes, short curly hair, and birdlike face and body. An aspiring writer, she sought my advice about doing travel pieces, which I sweetly and sagely gave her.

I was trying to think how I could get Tony to go out of town so I could have more freedom to pursue my new hobby. At this point, I was leaving for work at six o'clock in the morning so I could stop at Sean's house on the way in. I was riding a bicycle all over the place, just like he did, and wearing a little silver hoop earring in my ear, just like he did, and carrying a black backpack, just like he did.

One evening during dinner—a lovely meal of mesquite-grilled chicken salad and homemade focaccia I'd spent hours on, in the grand tradition of lovely meals served to cheated-on partners by their suddenly-so-solicitous spouses—I casually suggested to Tony that he might like to take a little break from the household routine. I'll be fine, I said, just like when you were at the spa.

I was surprised at how quickly he snapped it up. He said he'd been thinking of going to New Orleans to visit his friend Kathryn. Kathryn was a woman in her mid-forties, a rather unusual person he had met at a nightclub in Austin through their mutual friends on the industrial music scene. Several years earlier, she'd moved to New Orleans with her husband, an older Jimmy Stewart type who'd made a lot of money in the commodities market and who'd met Kathryn when she subbed for his regular girl at the massage parlor. There was something about her that had always bothered me. For one thing, ever since she'd moved, Tony and she maintained a weird arrangement where she would send him money and he would buy her pot and FedEx it back to her. I thought this was ridiculous. Why couldn't she buy her own pot? In New Orleans, of all places? It seemed like a lot of hassle and risk for no good reason.

However, I wasn't too concerned about any of this at that moment. I kissed him goodbye and sent him merrily on his way.

While he was gone, I saw Sean almost as much as I wanted, except I could have been with him every minute and not seen him as much as I wanted. And part of the time, his girlfriend was back in town. But when the coast was clear, he would come over to see me after the kids were asleep. One night I was curled up on the couch reading and I heard him playing his harmonica out in my backyard. I got up and went out to him, standing in front of him, almost trembling. The last note of the song hung in the air as he pulled me down to him, weaving his fingers through my hair, wrapping his arms around me. He stood up, lifting me as if I were weightless, and carried me across the deck to the chaise longue.

It was quite a week. I cooked him dinner, we went to the movies (could it really have been *The Unforgiven?*), I asked him to watch my kids while I went to a meeting at the *Chronicle*. At four and two, they were not old enough to wonder who the hell he was and why he was suddenly around so much. He was good with them, like a counselor at summer camp.

Anyway, I wasn't worried about what people thought, not even my kids. I didn't feel guilty; I was too busy floating. Whereas before I was famous at work for shuffling back and forth to and from the coffeepot with my head down, ignoring everyone, now I was Miss Congeniality, smiling and saying hi and chitchatting, wearing sexy outfits instead of the same blue jeans every day. I lost thirty pounds in about three weeks because I hardly ate and I never slept because I had to stay up all night thinking what to wear to work the next day and composing seductive E-mail messages in my head. Exhilarated, I didn't care who knew; I was a walking advertisement and every word out of my mouth was a double entendre.

One night that week, Sean and I took my kids out for pizza. After dinner, we dropped him at his house. After I'd put the kids in the tub, I noticed the light on the message machine was flashing. I pressed PLAYBACK, waited for the creaky rewind, then heard, over the background static of an outdoor pay phone, the voice of our friend Sue from New Orleans.

I have some bad news, Marion, she said. Tony's been arrested. He's in jail here in New Orleans. I don't have much information, but it's something with drugs—heroin, I believe. It sounds pretty serious. Call me as soon as you get in.

I was gasping for breath as if I'd been kicked in the stomach, but the kids were in the tub and I knew I had to get them to sleep before I could even replay the message, much less give way to the panic I felt coming on. I was so upset, I could barely remember where the bathroom was.

What's the matter, Mommy? said Hayes. He had formed his lathered hair into Batman-style pointy ears, while his little brother wore the creation they referred to as "Eiffel Tower."

Oh nothing, sweetie, Mommy's just a little tired, I said carefully, supporting Hayes's neck with one hand as I poured the rinse water over his head from a large plastic cup.

Are you crying? asked Vincie, his eyes round and blue as Wedgwood plates.

No, honey. Come on, here's your towel. It's late.

Story! Story! they clamored as we proceeded to the bedroom.

Just one story, boys. Here, put on your sleep shirts and get in bed.

Thank God they fell asleep halfway through *Worse Than Rotten Ralph*.

When I called Sue back, she knew very little beyond what she'd said on the machine—no specifics on where Tony was or what he'd been charged with, no way for me to get in touch with him. He was "in the system." Sue promised me that in the morning she'd use her connections at the police department to find out more.

The next message on the tape after Sue was Kerry Jaggers, another friend of Tony's from the industrial-music crowd. He'd left his pager number and said to get in touch with him right away. When he returned my page, he said he already knew about the bust, and told me to meet him at a gay bar downtown if I wanted to talk. I got a friend to come over and stay with the boys so I could go.

If they wake up, I told her, just tell them I went to the 7-Eleven to get some milk. Lie down with them for a while and sing "Sweet Baby James" and they'll go back to sleep.

I threaded my way through the shirtless couples on the dance floor and found Kerry at a table on the patio out back, a backwards cap on his shaved head and several acolytes hanging around. He sent them away, gave me a hug, and ordered me a drink. He had no more details about the arrest, but he told me that Kathryn was a longtime junkie and she and Tony had begun getting high together when they first met three years earlier. The "pot" she had been sending money for all this time was heroin— I guess like me, a decade earlier, she could never find any in New Orleans. According to Kerry, the shipments had been far more frequent that I had realized, and what Tony got out of it, I now saw, was free drugs.

Now it looked like Tony had been doing heroin since before Vince was born. I couldn't believe it. Though it certainly did explain why I would catch him nodding out over dinner every once in a while, those *Gaslight* experiences where he easily convinced me to doubt the evidence of my own eyes. And it also helped to explain what he was doing with all that coke the year before; it made much more sense that he was doing speedballs— mixing the cocaine and heroin together—than shooting the coke straight.

Kerry bought me one drink after another as I chain-smoked

and cried on his shoulder. As freaked out as I was about the length and breadth of Tony's deception, my overriding concern was to get him out of jail. If only to make him explain to me what the hell was going on.

In the days following, all I could think of to say to myself was, Okay, Marion, if you can't handle it, next time don't marry a junkie faggot with AIDS. In my deranged state, I thought that was just hilarious.

Sue called to tell me the details of the arrest: Kathryn and Tony had had some heroin FedExed to them from New York, and the DEA had caught it in a routine drug check at the airport. They had followed the delivery truck to the house; a whole crew of agents in their DEA baseball caps and jackets busted in as Kathryn was cooking up her stuff in the bathroom. Tony was in the living room waiting his turn. It was the use of Federal Express that automatically made their charge distribution instead of just possession—ironic, after all these years of its functioning as our private drug delivery service.

Each of them had been charged with intent to distribute heroin, a charge that carried a mandatory life sentence in Louisiana. Typical bail for such an offense was $300,000.

What should I do? I asked her. I was in shock. I had just swept a whole pile of folded laundry off the bed and now was picking it up and mechanically refolding it, the portable phone cradled under my ear.

I should come there, I said. But the kids, my job—I don't know how fast I can get out of town.

There's nothing you can do right now, Marion, she replied. You probably can't even see him. Anyway, you don't want to upset the kids any more than you have to. What you need to do is sit tight and hire a lawyer.

Why can't you be our lawyer? I asked her.

I'm not a criminal lawyer, she said. You need someone with a lot of drug experience. This is serious, you don't want to mess around.

Who's the best? I asked.

She gave me his number.

But you saw Tony, right? How's he doing? Is he okay?

Well, he told them he had AIDS, so he got put in the gay section of the jail, which is by far the less rough and dangerous. He's pretty freaked out, of course. He asked me to get him some cigarettes, and he was worried about his medicine. He was arrested under the name Heubach because that's how his fingerprints came up, and the prescription bottles all said Winik, so they took them away.

That's ridiculous, I said. He has all kinds of ID that says Winik.

Well, I don't think he showed that ID when he got arrested. I think he was hoping at first that this was all going to blow over fast. That's probably why he didn't phone you when they let him make his one phone call. In fact, when he got in touch with me, he asked me not to tell you about it.

Not to tell me about it? *Not to tell me about it?* Jesus Christ, I said. He's nuts.

Well, he knows you know now. He said when I talk to you again, tell you hi.

Hi, I said weakly. Tell him I said hi too. Tell him I'll get him a lawyer and figure out something about the prescriptions. I can't call him? Can I write him a letter or something?

Yes, sure, fax it to my office and I'll get it to him.

Oh God, Sue, I said. Can you believe all this? That poor crazy baby.

When's Daddy coming home? Hayes asked me a few days later when I picked the boys up from school. Vincie was too little to pay attention to grown-up conversations, but Hayes had heard enough to know that something was wrong. I wanted to be as honest as possible without giving him more information than he could handle. He was too young to even know what drugs were. I had called a child psychologist who was a client of Tony's to get some advice; she said she'd get back to me, but in fact she never called again, not even for a hair appointment.

I'm not sure exactly when he's coming home, Hayes, I told him, making my voice steady. He's in jail.

What's jail? he asked. I'm sure he had seen jails in cartoons, but had no idea how those images corresponded to real life.

It's something like time-out, I said. When you break the rules and you have to go in time-out for a while.

How long? Five minutes?

Not five minutes. Longer. A person called a lawyer helps you work it out. You have to say you're sorry.

Can I call Daddy?

Not right now. If he can't come home soon, we'll go visit him. Don't worry, sweetie. Everything's going to be okay.

Can Vincie and me have a Popsicle?

What? Can you have a Popsicle? Sure, honey.

My explanation and reassurances seemed to satisfy Hayes; I wished they did the same for me. I felt like I was having a nervous breakdown. I really thought Tony might be locked up for life, might die of AIDS in jail, might never play with his children or sleep in our bed again. At night, after I put the kids down, I would drink glass after glass of wine, smoke cigarette after cigarette, make phone call after phone call. Images of prison visits, strained meetings over picnic tables in exercise yards, reeled through my mind. I had no idea how to put together the astronomical bail. I was trying to avoid telling either my mother or Tony's anything until I actually knew what was going on. The lawyer was my only hope, and he wasn't too encouraging so far.

Sean was around some that week, trying to overlook the bizarreness of the situation and be a friend to me. One night, the kids stayed at a friend's house and I asked him to sleep over. Then I started crying so hard in bed it was all he could do to calm me down.

He's a part of me, Tony's a part of me, I wailed. It's like a part of me is in jail in Louisiana. I can't stand it, I can't stand it. What can I do?

Sean was very sweet and brave in the face of this hysteria, talking to me softly, trying everything he could think of to get me to relax. His kindness made a deep impression on me, and made things much harder for me later on.

NO MAGIC

Tony was saved from doom by a combination of political finagling and pure dumb luck, in what proportion I am not sure to this day. The lawyer I'd hired contributed a large part of the $3,500 retainer I'd sent him to the district attorney's reelection campaign. He and the D.A. were old schoolmates. The two of them went down to the evidence room, had the cop on duty bring out the dope that had been confiscated from Kathryn and Tony, and personally walked it through the testing process, which would normally have taken up to three weeks.

The tests showed that the drugs were bogus. The dealer had ripped them off, and by doing so, saved their asses. There was no evidence. Our lawyer and the D.A. went down to talk to the judge and Tony and Kathryn were released more or less immediately.

There are a few things that bug me about this story. If the dealer was going to rip them off, why did he bother sending the FedEx package at all? And if the drugs were not real, why did the DEA dogs at the airport get so excited about the smell of the package? Did the contribution to the district attorney's reelection pay for a fake report from testing? Even if the drugs were fake, isn't the criminal intent still there? Or did the state of Louisiana just decide to send this particular junkie faggot with AIDS back home to Texas instead of supporting him in jail for the rest of his life?

Looking back at the letters Tony wrote me from jail, which are filled with repentance and fear and incredible longing for the

everyday—"I dream of holding you, playing with the kids, cleaning the house, taking my morning walk, eating some watermelon, swimming, cleaning the pool, watering the flowers,
mowing the lawn"—I wonder if things would have been different if I hadn't just lost my mind over Sean. If the timing had been
better, would we have gotten the fresh start Tony was pleading
for and looking forward to in those letters? If I had had the energy to try to start over, would Tony have stuck to his resolve to
get help and quit drugs?

Sadly, my detachment from the relationship was a long-term
development of which Sean was a symptom rather than a cause.
I had finally woken up from my self-induced trance of okayness
and suddenly nothing was okay. It wasn't just that we didn't have
sex; our whole life now looked to me like a web of power trips
and dependency. We could hardly have an honest conversation or
a decent argument. No trust, no communication, no real intimacy.

The last time I talked to Tony on the phone before he came
home from New Orleans—he was out of jail, resting up at Sue's
before the drive back—I told him he had to stop lying to me.

Then you stop lying too, he said. Are you having an affair?

I saw no way around admitting I had slept with Sean. By this
time, his girlfriend had come home and the pressure of the situation was too much for him. He had told me we shouldn't see
each other anymore.

I slept with Sean Spencer, I confessed to Tony. But it's over
now. We'll talk about it when you get home. Just come home,
okay?

He did. I was sitting in the yard, watching the kids splash
each other in the pool, when he walked in the back gate. He was
emaciated, beaten, and dead-eyed, moving like an old man. And
even as my heart went out to him, as I jumped from the chair

and went to him, I knew: I loved Tony, but I wasn't in love with him anymore.

I was crying as much about that as everything else as we stood there, holding each other, tears pouring down both our faces, soon joined by the kids, who finally looked up from their game and saw he was there. Daddy! they shouted, and ran up the hill to throw their dripping little bodies into his arms. He was so weak, they almost knocked him over.

For weeks he barely talked at all. When he did, he'd tell half-funny, half-horrible stories about jail, the conditions, the other inmates, the clothes, the television outside his cell that was always on, invariably showing B movies about prison. His health was slipping; jail had quickly reversed all the improvements inspired by the spa. He was in pain of some kind all the time—muscle aches, headaches, his legs hurt, he had diarrhea. He had trouble sleeping, and his night sweats, which had been a problem for years, were worse than ever—the sheets and pillow were soaked every morning.

Dr. Benito put him on antidepressants and gave him Klonopin to help him sleep. In response to his many aches and pains, he continued to prescribe Tylenol with codeine, which Tony began to swallow like candy. Exactly when he began doing street drugs again, I'm not sure.

I was in some pain myself, unable to stop thinking about Sean and the pleasure and happiness I had had during our interlude together. But no matter what I said or did, he was steadfast in his insistence that we could only be friends. In September, he left town for three months and my grief over his departure was so out of proportion to the circumstances, I didn't need a shrink to figure it out. Instead of mourning for my messed-up, dying husband, I would weep for my supple and perfect young lover who was out of town and who didn't want to sleep with me anymore. As much as this hurt, at least it was a hurt I was familiar with.

A few weeks later, we took the boys up north for Labor Day weekend. Tony was still very weak; the day my mom and Nancy and I took Hayes and Vince to the Bronx Zoo, he stayed at Nancy's apartment to rest. While we were gone, he went through my purse and found a journal I had been keeping. It recorded my feelings about Sean, my attempts to untangle myself from my addiction to him, my despair as I told myself again and again that the affair was over.

Tony's reading this was the worst thing that could possibly have happened. Up to then, he had not been aware of the intensity of my emotions about Sean, the details of the affair, or, most horribly, the degree to which our own romance had faded for me. Naturally, I had tried to conceal all this from him. So why didn't I hide the journal more carefully? Was I trying to get caught? Did I want him to know the things I couldn't bear to tell him? I'm sure that's what a psychologist would suggest, but it's also true that at that time I really wasn't used to keeping secrets and hiding things and being spied on. It wouldn't have occurred to me that Tony would go through my purse and look at every piece of paper in it. Soon I would have a password on my computer and a clear understanding that I was under surveillance all the time.

In Tony's mind, my betrayal far outweighed his. He had gotten caught with drugs, big deal. I had fallen in love with someone else. This filled him with jealousy and anger and, strangely, lust. Suddenly, he wanted me. But now it was I who failed to respond, I who returned tentative overtures with sisterly affection. Soon the overtures stopped and he would just rail about my unwillingness to have sex.

This is too much, he would moan. With everything else that's happened to me, now I can't even have sex with my wife?

It was too late. After all the years of rejection, my desire for Tony had virtually disappeared. I had been forced to accept, over the years, that sex was not a big part of our relationship, and I *had* accepted it. I couldn't even make myself believe in the desire he now professed for me; it seemed just a way of scrambling to own me again. My view was that we should try to reinvent our coupledom based on what we did share; we could still live together, be friends, raise the kids—and have sex with other people.

He said this was completely unacceptable, only the monogamous arangement we had agreed to in the first place would do.

His testosterone surge, frustrated, turned to rage; his physical overtures, to violence. The first fight I remember occurred right after he found the journal, on that same vacation up north. We were at Liz Lambert and her girlfriend Margaret's apartment in Brooklyn—they had moved up there after finishing law school at the University of Texas a few years earlier. Now Liz was nearing the end of a three-year stint as an assistant D.A. in New York; she lived right around the corner from Sandye. It should have been a great night, a reunion with old friends, drinking, eating take-out Chinese food, talking. But we drank too much, ate too little, and talked too bitterly. Liz, who had a trial in the morning, pleaded exhaustion and went up to bed, leaving Margaret and Sandye to watch helplessly as the hostilities escalated.

Everything's my fault, you see, I was explaining, my voice twisted with sarcasm and pain. It's even my fault that he went to jail, because without me, he would never have done heroin in the first place. And of course my affair is my fault; my deception about that knocks out his four years of lying to me. Whatever isn't my fault—and this is a very small category—is AIDS' fault. So that's it. He's perfect.

As I was speaking, Tony came up behind me, slipped my purse off the back of my chair and dumped its contents on my head. Not quite grasping what was going on for a moment, I continued right on talking as pencils and lipsticks and coins began to rain down on my shoulders. I remember seeing Margaret's eyes widen, her hand fly to her mouth.

I jumped up and tried to grab the purse away from him; he shoved me away and we fell on each other like cats. Because Tony was not all that threatening physically and because I thought I sensed limits to how much he would or could hurt me, during the first few fights we had I would fight back rather than run, which resulted in some confusion about whose "fault" the incidents were.

That night, we wrestled on the floor until suddenly I saw blood on my shirt. There was a cut on the side of my face where some sharp edge of his jewelry had split the skin. I screamed and struggled out of his grip.

Okay, guys, said Sandye shakily. Time out.

Tony stalked to the door, winging a cold, hard eggroll at me as he slammed out into the street. I cried inconsolably in Margaret's arms while Sandye went to look for him.

In the morning, we were too hungover and embarrassed to be angry. We sat drinking Sandye's strong coffee and trying to make jokes as blurry images of the night before took shape in our heads. But it was easier for us to apologize to our friends than to each other, and in our hearts, the campfires of resentment burned on.

Back in Texas, we went into marriage counseling with a woman psychologist recommended by some friends who were going through a divorce. Tony was not too enthusiastic about the idea; he had never had much interest in therapy. Since I didn't think he would have the patience to interview several different doctors, I had to hope this woman would be right for us.

She wasn't, or perhaps we were just beyond this sort of help. Tony was enraged to the point of violence in many of the sessions; he walked out of more than one of them, too angry to talk about his anger. If he wasn't shouting or walking out, he was sitting there mute—when she asked him about his father, about the violence in his childhood, he shut down completely. He felt that she was inexperienced with AIDS and terminal illness, that she couldn't understand his situation. She had a mixed metaphor she used frequently about all the pieces of the jigsaw puzzle being up in the air that drove him crazy. After a while, I felt like I was paying ninety dollars an hour just to have someone agree with me—yes, I'm at the end of my rope, yes, he's out of control.

I think it's so funny how the minute we hear of anyone having problems these days, the first question is always, Is she in counseling? Is he getting help? Like it's magic or something. It's not. Sometimes it even makes things worse, all the bad stuff being dredged up from the bottom on an arbitrary schedule when maybe things have finally begun to settle down.

Still, I kept trying to get some "support," as everyone kept telling me I should. After we gave up on the marriage counselor, we had a preliminary session with a therapist at a local AIDS resource center. By this time, things were so explosive that Tony stormed out of the first meeting, the tails of his linen shirt flying, necklaces banging against his chest, and walked the whole four miles back to our house.

I continued to see her by myself for several years. She was very gentle and supportive; I needed that. Tony later saw a peer counselor at the same resource center—this must have been a concession after some new explosion of the continuing crisis— but I never knew what they talked about, or if Tony told him the truth, and then the guy moved out of town.

I also joined an HIV wives' support group that year, every Wednesday during lunch for a couple of months. Everyone was black except for me and one fundamentalist Christian woman whose husband said the devil made him go to the gay dirty book-store. And now God was going to take his AIDS away. Another woman had had a hysterectomy and the doctor told her she couldn't have sex for six months. So her husband started catting around, and now he had AIDS and expected her to wait on him hand and foot.

My last husband, she told us ominously, I shot his dick off.

I guess this solution occurs to people more than you would think.

It was interesting, but it wasn't exactly support. Sometimes when you're alone, you're just alone. All the psychosocial creativity of the late twentieth century can't do a thing for you.

DISNEY WORLD

For Christmas, Tony's mother planned a family trip to Disney World. Though it would surely be fun for the kids, I was filled with trepidation. Grace and I had reached an all-time low in our relationship over that Labor Day visit during which Tony read my journal, the final disaster of which occurred during the weekend we spent at her house in Lansdale.

Though I had concealed the jail incident from his mother, as I knew he would want me to, I was tired of all the secrets. Tony's health was declining, his drug problem was getting worse, our marriage was in trouble, and it was just not possible to go on pretending. I wanted him to tell her, if not everything all at once, at least about AIDS, and he had agreed to do it while we were visiting.

Though part of my reason for demanding this was for her sake and his, part of it was for me. Grace was the only other person in the world who cared for Tony as much as I did, who loved him unconditionally. Having her involved would spread things out a little, I felt, would take some of the weight off me.

Whatever the outcome, I had determined that the time had come for her to know that Tony had AIDS. But since our arrival Friday night, we had been busy with dinner at his grandmother's, miniature golf with the cousins, shopping expeditions for school clothes. I had made an excuse not to go on the shopping trip, thinking maybe he would find the time to tell her then, but when they got back, he said, Are you kidding? In the mall? With the kids?

Sunday morning, I woke up at 6 A.M. in the basement room
we were sharing with the boys. I looked over at Tony and knew
he was never going to get up the nerve to tell her. So I put on a
T-shirt and jeans and marched upstairs to the kitchen to wait for
her to wake up.

She was already standing at the counter, dealing with last
night's dishes and starting to fix breakfast. She made pancake
batter, beat eggs, fried bacon, washed berries, and mixed up orange juice, so she could make each person exactly what they
wanted when they woke up.

Good morning, she said.

Good morning. Oh, can I have some coffee?

Take some.

So, Grace, I began, pacing around a little, I have to tell you
something. I wanted Tony to tell you, but I'm afraid he can't
bring himself to do it, and I thought maybe if I just broke the ice,
you two could talk about it. It's been going on a long time and I
wanted him to tell you before, but he said he didn't want you to
worry, but it's really too much what with all that's been going
on, and, well, Tony has AIDS. He's had it for a long time, we're
pretty sure he was HIV-positive when we met, he's been doing
great so far, but lately things haven't been so great and I thought
it was time for you to know.

Grace had her back to me while I delivered my speech, and
when she turned around, her eyebrows were one straight line
and her lips were pressed together.

Tony and I will talk about this when he gets up, she said.

I'm sorry, I said, I wanted him to tell you, but—

Marion, she said sharply, I don't want to talk about this with
you anymore. Tony and I will talk when he gets up.

She turned back to her mixing bowl.

I was on the verge of tears, clutching my coffee cup, exploding with things to say. But that was it, no more talking. I went downstairs.

Tony, I said, shaking his shoulder, wake up.

He shrugged me off and burrowed into the pillow. What?

I told her.

Immediately his eyes flew open. You did what?

I told her. I didn't tell her much, just that you have AIDS and you've had it for a long time. She wants to talk to you.

Oh, goddamn it. He rubbed his forehead with the heel of his palm and reached for his cigarettes.

Later that day, Tony and Grace went out somewhere in the car. When they returned, he told me their conversation had gone pretty well, considering. She was totally uninformed about AIDS, had asked a million questions, and was planning to make an appointment with her doctor to get more information.

Was she upset? Did she cry?

Of course she was upset. What do you think?

That was about all he told me. The rest of that day was difficult; Grace was giving me the cold shoulder as never before. Or maybe she was just upset and that was her way of acting and I was taking it too personally. That evening, before we left, I bought some dopey "You're Special to Me" card at the drugstore and wrote a note to her inside it. The note said that I was sorry for what had happened, that I cared for and respected her and Rod, but that I was tired of feeling disapproved of and even disliked all the time. Since, I pointed out, I was financially supporting and otherwise taking care of her son and her grandsons, didn't I deserve a little support? We may be very different, but we're stuck with each other, and I can't stand to feel this way anymore.

You can just imagine how this note went over. But the fact is, I had already begun avoiding Grace and Rod because of feeling this way. When they'd come down to visit over Easter earlier that year, I went out of town for the weekend with a bunch of my girlfriends. When we were up north, I looked for ways to shorten our visits. By writing the note, I was trying to get things off this bad track.

Maybe that was Grace's idea too, when she set up this jaunt to Disney World. But there were so many factors weighing against its working out, it was unbelievable. For one thing—surprise!—all six of us were staying in one room, a crowded room with two double beds in the Dixie Landings part of the Disney resort, where Muzak versions of "Song of the South," "Old Man River," and, of course, "Dixie," were continuously piped in through outdoor microphones. For another thing, Tony was completely tanked on Valium and Vicodin the entire time, walking around the Magic Kingdom like a zombie, and ate so many of the pills so quickly that he had to take to his bed on the fourth day of the trip, complaining of muscle aches in his legs and feet. He called Benito's office and had them phone in a refill to an Orlando pharmacy. To explain why a two-week supply was already gone, he told the nurse his luggage had been lost by the airline.

His mother was so worried about his "pain"—I thought of it in quotes—I figured I'd let her pick up the tab on this one. Though I didn't doubt that his physical complaints were authentic, and that the drugs made them easier to bear, his way of using them went far beyond pain control. He just wanted to be blasted all the time. To do this, he continually exceeded his dosages, ran out of pills, and staged one medical emergency after the next to get everyone else involved in helping him score. Even when you know the person has an AIDS diagnosis, and is suffering on many levels, you can only go through this so many times without hardening to it. Especially because I couldn't help thinking that he would be more functional if he would just stop taking all that shit.

I am sorry to admit the following little bit of hypocrisy, but the fact is that throughout that ghastly week in Disney World, I would eagerly swallow any pills he chose to dole out to me, or I happened to find spilled in the bottom of the videocamera case. The way things were going, I felt I needed as much anesthesia and instant euphoria as anyone else.

Things between Tony and me were bad, very bad, though in our own futile, off-and-on ways, we were trying. By this time, Sean had been out of town for several months, and even though I was thinking about him, I was also trying to pull my family life together, finding those moments when everything was how it used to be and holding on as long as I could. Tony was similarly at cross-purposes: taking more and more pills and being sullen and moody, while trying to recapture that dream of home life he had had in jail. We kept trying to love each other, to refind our balance.

Unfortunately, Tony had become extremely suspicious and was always searching through my drawers, my purse, looking over the credit-card bills and the phone bill and any papers I left lying around. One day, he came to surprise me at work for lunch, and when he found I was out, he searched my office. He found an old driver's license of Sean's and some of his mail stuck in one of my desk drawers. He waited for me to get back, then as soon I got there, started swearing at me and screaming at me, pushing me up against the wall and acting like he was going to hit me, though he didn't, then stormed out with the letters and license crumpled into a ball in his fist.

By the time I got home, he had built a bonfire of Sean's things in a metal Dallas Cowboys garbage pail and was packing to leave. I found this letter on the kitchen table:

You are giving me the impression that maintaining your friendship with Sean is more important than our marriage. And it's something I can't deal with I walk around with this queasy feeling in my guts. I know that I should not look to the past or to the future and just be happy for the now, but I can't. Maybe you should be free for him when he returns—who knows, one thing I do know is that all this shit has taken an incredible toll on my physical and emotional health and maybe we should take a break from each other and see how we feel then. I've been honest with you about my feelings and what would ease some of my insecurities and you've given me your answer so I don't know what else to do at this point I'm really sorry

I love you

P.S. you need to work out your feelings about this—your relationship with Sean and with me. I know you love me, but with me you can't have your cake and eat it too it's Sean or me sorry. Mar I love you immensely I can't watch you be so torn about this. This is something I never thought would happen in our relationship, but it has and I hate it. I just can't handle any more of your secret feelings. I know in your heart you think you should stay with me—for the kids sake and whatever other justifications you make for staying with me, but if you're not happy maybe you should think again or you're going to wonder what if for the rest of your life. I feel really sick about the lies and deceptions from both of us and I only want you to be happy and feel okay. Please don't freak about this I am just trying to be honest with myself and you I am very afraid to give you this Just know I love you

One minute he was hurting me and shouting at me, the next minute writing me heartrending love letters. I was feeling more worn out than anything else. I just wanted him to unpack the suitcase and sit down to dinner, rather than tear off into the night and pave the way for a new set of crises.

In my reply, I asked him not to go. I recited my catechism:

the boys need him, I need him, he needs us, our time is short, my affair is over. Try to ease up on this thing, I pleaded.

He didn't leave that day, but two weeks later, in the wake of another round of fighting, he took off in the car. I got a message on my answering machine a couple of days later that he was in Birmingham, Alabama, visiting that Tomé guy he'd been corresponding with since Mardi Gras. When I called the number he left, the person who answered acted like I had no business inquiring where Tomé and his out-of-town friend were, but eventually told me they'd gone out to the Love Shack, the number for which was 1-205-NOW-DIGM.

Well, well, well. Though my position vis-à-vis this vacation of Tony's was a little hard to figure out, I was more encouraged than outraged. If it would take the heat off me, I was for it. I made him promise, however, to come back in time for our outing to Disney World, so I wouldn't have to explain to his mother that he couldn't be with us because he was visiting his new boyfriend in the Love Shack.

So there we all were at Disney World, on top of each other every second, from five o'clock in the morning when we had to get up and get to the park to take advantage of their letting guests staying "on property" in early, until late at night when we returned, all exhausted and cranky beyond belief. The mood was tense, with all of us focusing on the kids to avoid dealing with each other.

One night, I was trying to put the boys to sleep. Trying, but not succeeding. The lights were on, Grace and Rod were sitting at the table reading, Tony was outside smoking cigarettes and nodding out. Hayes and Vince were wired and overtired in the way that children can be only after a full day at an amusement park, playing games that involved a lot of jumping on the beds and shouting and had one or the other in tears every five minutes. I had a backache, a headache, and absolutely no patience left, having spent fourteen hours in the broiling Florida sun dealing with their whims, including carrying Vince on my shoulders for an hour when he got too tired to walk, with no help from his father. I took a very, very deep breath.

Come on boys, let's get in bed. I'll read you a story.

Hayes continued jumping on the bed as if I had said nothing.

Here, hold the book, Vincie, I said, and got up to physically drag Hayes to bed.

As I struggled with Hayes, Vince slipped out of the sheets on the other side.

Get back in bed, Vincie.

I have to pee.

Hurry up.

Vince came back, they cuddled up on either side of me, and I opened the book.

Once upon a time there was a little bunny—

I need my Goofy, interrupted Hayes.

You do not need your Goofy.

I WANT MY GOOFY, he started to wail.

Dozens of plastic figures and toys were scattered across the floor of the room, along with discarded clothes and extra bedding.

Well, forget it. I can't find your Goofy right now. Do you want to hear this story or not?

Here's your Goofy, Hayes, said Grace, handing it to him.

That's *my* Goofy, Vince shouted.

I pulled them apart and threw Goofy across the room. Forget the story. Could we turn off the light, please? Just lie still.

As soon as the lights were off, I, at least, began to fall asleep. Then Hayes began kicking me under the covers.

Lie still, Hayes, I hissed.

He continued to wriggle around, I continued to hiss, until finally in the course of rolling over, he elbowed me in the eye.

Goddamn it, I shouted, sitting up and smacking him in the arm.

Grace flicked on the light immediately. You cannot treat these children this way, she said. If you're too tired, I'll put them to bed.

Treat these children what way? I asked. What way?

She picked up the book, cleared her throat, and started to read: The bunny's mother said, If you become a sailboat, I'll become a warm wind and blow you home again.

I went outside with a lump in my throat to bum a cigarette from my zombie.

After the kids were asleep, I asked Grace to explain exactly what she thought I was doing wrong. You make it sound like I'm a child-abuser or something, I said.

I don't want to talk about it, she said.

You never want to talk about anything, I replied bitterly.

Marion, she said in a choked voice, I have not slept since September. I have had a continuous stomachache. I am sick about what's going on, and I think everything that needs to be said has already been said.

With that, she got up and hurried out of the room. I followed her, but she seemed so hell-bent on escaping me, speeding across the manicured lawns of Dixie Landings, dodging between the topiary Br'er Rabbit bushes, that finally I gave up and let her go.

Why does she hate me, I sobbed to my father-in-law, who had taken this opportunity to come out on the "porch" and light one of his secret cigarettes. Why does she hate me so much? It's not my fault she hasn't slept since September. It's not my fault Tony has AIDS.

Taking a long, deep drag of his cigarette, he just rocked back and forth on the wicker chair as if he hadn't heard me.

Well, that was it. I gave up. The last few days at the park, I would trudge along a few steps behind Grace, a little ditty Tony had made up a few months earlier going through my head. *I hate you, you hate me, we're a dysfunctional family,* it began, sung to the tune of the theme song from "Barney and Friends." There I'd be, lifting Hayes and Vincie into a Dumbo cart, or helping them up the mast of the pirate ship, or settling a skirmish over which was Chip and which was Dale, and every minute my little tape loop would be playing.

The highlight of the whole godforsaken experience was New Year's Eve, when Tony and I ditched the kids at the Peter Pan Club, lost the in-laws at the Tiki Lounge, and met a bunch of friends from southern Florida who had an annual ritual of dropping acid on New Year's Eve at Disney World. That night, tripping my ass off, hanging on Tony, sitting in his lap, giggling all over Space Mountain and the Haunted Mansion and Pirates of the Caribbean—with the help of psychedelics, the Kingdom was finally Magic to me. It was like the olden days, drugs bringing us together instead of driving us apart, our closeness the one solid thing in a world that was not quite real.

After the park closed, we went back to our friends' condominium to drink champagne. I sat dazzle-eyed and grinning, a bottle of Moët between my knees, as my still-beautiful ice-skater twirled in his stocking feet on the polished hardwood floor, his arms swooping, his fingers trailing stars, showing us the things he used to do.

SEPARATE WAYS

The last day at Disney World, I was playing with the kids at the Yacht Club Caribbean Beach Resort, which had a mammoth swimming pool with a real sand bottom and a shipwrecked galleon with water slides protruding from it in every direction.

Look at me, Mommy. Look! Are you looking? Mommy!

I'm looking, I'm looking, I swear.

It was the day Sean was supposed to be back in the office after coming home from Central America. As soon as Tony left the pool for a while, I went to the phone and called him.

It was January, we hadn't slept together since August, and he had been telling me nothing but to forget it ever since. Well, not quite. There were a few mixed messages, such as the turquoise-and-black handwoven dress he brought me from Guatemala, which he had to hide from his girlfriend and I couldn't even take home because Tony would have known what it was if he saw it in my closet.

A two-week-long sexual relationship, several hundred E-mail messages, thousands of words in journals and letters, twelve months of my life down a black hole of obsession and craving. I made Sean hurt me over and over and over again. I don't know whether the purpose was to make progress toward the goal of letting go of him or whether I just liked being in misery and making a fool of myself. I went to see him play with his band at the Hole in the Wall one night, and the sound of his harmonica seemed to be everything about him: Wyoming, his youth and casualness, his very good heart. I sat in the audience with tears dripping down my face, but couldn't even go up and talk to him because his girlfriend was there. Everybody kept telling me I looked beautiful. It must have been a combination of the anguish and the Guatemalan dress.

I was talking about everything all the time; talking was the valve to release the pressure. I would tell people about Sean, about Tomé, about Tony's illness, about the drugs, about his hitting me. This last was always the big news with the predictable reaction: Oh my God, you've got to leave, you're a battered wife.

I brushed off this advice every time I heard it, though I had begun to feel very frightened of Tony's violent eruptions and no longer so sure about the limits of what he would do. One night when we were coming home from a party, arguing all the way because he was so loaded and kept denying it and then turned it around, started screaming about my lying to him. On the path down to the house, he shoved me into the nandina bushes and stood over me with his face twisted and shouting, kicking me. I lay scratched and bleeding in the bushes until I saw a chance to get away. We had a male baby-sitter that night and I thought if I could just get into the house and sit near him, I would be safe.

Are you all right? the baby-sitter asked. What happened?

Oh, nothing, I said. I'm just a little out of breath.

Where's Tony?

He's, um, on his way in.

After a few minutes, I realized Tony must have gone back out in the car, so I sent the sitter home and went to bed. I lay there with the light on, staring up at the ceiling fan, knowing his threatening me physically was wrong, but with no idea at all of how to stop it. I was determined to stay with him no matter what. That was my commitment. Through sickness and health, through better and worse. Just like I promised.

Tony's physical condition was determined more and more by his inventory of pain pills and tranquilizers. If he had a good supply, he was fine. When he ran out, he was a mess. A pharmacist complained to Benito about how frequently Tony was coming in for refills; Ray talked to him about getting off Valium and codeine. That lasted about a week. Aches, pains, diarrhea, coughing, and shortness of breath continued to plague him. He was losing weight, he was depressed, he was babbling in his sleep and sweating rivers every night.

At this point, Tony had what Benito called multisystem advanced AIDS. Although the virus had been wearing away at his strong constitution for years, his body was putting up a fierce fight. He had yet to spend a whole day in bed or suffer anything serious enough to put him in a hospital. Depression and drug addiction were proving to be the controlling factors in his decline. Yet I suppose there didn't seem much point in depriving him of the pills that were his only solace.

Part of me was disgusted with his constantly sedating himself; part of me understood; part of me wanted to do the same. Only rarely was I able to think past the awful mess of the current situation and say to myself, He is dying.

And then I would be knocked over with the agony of having to lose him, and always my next thought would be the boys. Thinking of them losing their father filled me with not just sorrow, but rage and fear. My poor, poor babies. This was not the story I wanted for them, but I was helpless to change it, helpless to prevent this cruel event from leaving its unimaginable mark on their lives.

And that would lead me back to being angry about drugs. Because of the drugs, they were losing him already.

In contrast to the increasing chaos and disaster at home, things were looking up for my writing. In January, I received the fellowship I'd applied for and signed with a literary agent who had heard me on the radio. In February, she sold a collection of my essays to a publisher in New York, and I cut down to three days a week at work. I needed time to finish my manuscript and I finally had the money to do it.

We never even had to discuss whether we would go to Guanajuato or not, as had once been the plan if I got the grant. The idea of taking our disintegrating family unit away from all the support systems that held it together—Tony's doctor and pharmacist, the kids' preschool and baby-sitters, my therapist and my paycheck and my telephone—seemed almost fantastic. To be marooned with Tony and the kids in a decrepit hacienda in a foreign country no longer appealed to me at all.

On February 8, 1993, Tony and I celebrated the ten-year anniversary of the day we met. Despite the sweet cards we exchanged that morning, I felt melancholy most of the day at work, listlessly answering my E-mails and drinking coffee. Then that afternoon, I was sitting in the backyard watching Hayes and Vince splash around in the hot tub with their friends Sarah and Laura Mallouk. Tony finished a haircut and came out to join us, tapping an unopened pack of Newports against the back of his hand before unwrapping it.

Having just watched *Sleeping Beauty* on videotape for the tenth time that week, the two girls were trying to entice the boys into playing Prince and Princess. *I know you,* they sang in high, giggling voices, *I walked with you once upon a dream. I know you, the gleam in your eyes is so familiar a gleam.*

Suddenly Tony rose from his chair, swept me into his arms and began to waltz me around the deck, continuing the song, whose lyrics we couldn't help but have memorized. *Yet I know it's true,* he serenaded in his off-key tenor, his eyes crinkled with humor and sparkling at me, *that visions are seldom all they seem.*

Helpless to resist, spurred on by the kids' hilarity, I joined in. *But if I know you, I know what you'll do. You'll love me at once, the way you did once upon a dream.* As we belted out the last words of the verse, Tony purposely danced us over the edge of the swimming pool, fully dressed and shod, his cigarette still burning between two fingers. The children could not believe their eyes.

Perhaps we still had something to celebrate after all.

I went to Colorado in March to perform one of my pieces for a new cable television show. I was so happy to get the hell away from everything; just to be alone in a hotel room or sit by myself in a café was like a dream come true. The day before I left town, Tony and I had had a nasty fight when I wondered how he'd managed to put 150 miles on the car in two days and he told me some story about going to a club the previous night. Not only was the club about three miles from our house, but his friends had called from there to ask if I knew where he was.

In the wake of the fight, he canceled two of his clients' appointments; he wasn't in the mood to cut hair. I was hysterical at the thought of his throwing away the chance to make forty dollars. Money was driving me crazy at this point, the concrete symbol of all the ways in which my life was out of control, the hot spring where my resentment and anger bubbled to the surface. Yes, yes, the boys, the house, the garden, the pool; he did all that, and all of it was for me. So I was obligated to take care of him and pay for everything and shut up about it. Right.

God only knew what he really was doing when he went out. I wasn't even sure I wanted to know. In some ways, I just wanted him to leave me alone and I would leave him alone and we could each do what we needed to do to make our lives bearable.

I wanted to stay together, I wanted to take care of him, but I didn't want to be in a straitjacket. Was there no way to drop our stranglehold on each other and live in civility and harmony? We were trapped, he in the victim role and I as the martyr, trapped in a marriage that had become dishonest and lonely, filled with manipulation, guilt, and fear. I could feel myself losing faith in my ability to be a good person, a decent parent, and any kind of wife.

The last night of the taping in Colorado, a British singer came in to record a musical segment for the show. Her piano player was a tough-looking Liverpool leather-jacket type who was transformed into an angel when he sang those ballads with her. I would say we knew we were going to sleep together almost immediately, and seven beers later we did, though he was a little concerned about my husband having AIDS and all.

Oh, don't worry about it, I told him as I ripped the buttons off his shirt.

I never saw this guy again, but he did call me once from San Francisco. I called him back, we talked, we said goodbye and good luck. A month later, Tony saw the unfamiliar San Francisco number on our phone bill and started his investigation, dialed the number and learned it was a motel, inquired whether the British musician had been registered there on the day of the call. He'd been suspicious ever since I got home from Colorado with a cassette tape of piano ballads by some guy he'd never heard of on a British recording label, and I must have looked at the picture on the liner too wistfully or played the tape once too often.

He called me at work, demanding to know what was going on.

Nothing, I told him.

You better stop lying to me, you fucking whore, he said, slamming the phone down at the other end.

It was lunchtime; the office was deserted as I paced the hall looking for someone to talk to or just be with. I was terrified. I honestly wondered if he might kill me if he found out I had been unfaithful again.

We cannot go on like this, I thought later that afternoon as I sat staring at the little clock on my computer screen, afraid to go home. He doesn't want to continue our marriage on my terms and I don't want to continue on his terms. I thought of all the times he'd tried to leave me and I'd stopped him; the last time I didn't try to stop him, but he didn't go anyway. I couldn't stand to hurt him and I couldn't stand that our marriage had failed, but I was hurting him and our marriage had failed, so what was the point? It was like living in an ugly house that you are embarrassed to bring people to; we had an ugly relationship and it was getting uglier by the minute. I felt like I should get down on my knees and pray for both of us and our boys; the situation was so out of control I imagined only God could help.

I left work a nervous wreck, picked up the kids, went home. I knew he wouldn't hit me in front of them.

Hayes and Vince ran ahead of me into the house, racing to the kitchen to get the cookies I'd told them were waiting. I was a few steps behind, shaking like a leaf, calling, Tony! We're home!

He was not in the house. I went out to look for him in the backyard, but he wasn't there either. Then I saw the cassette floating in the pool, the tape yanked from the cartridge.

He had drowned it.

TUNNEL OF LOVE

Nancy and Steve hadn't been in touch for almost a year when he called her in February 1993 to see if his C.P.A. ex-wife could spare five minutes from her busy life to help a dying man with his tax return. Happy to have a way to bridge the gap, knowing time was short, she drove in the next day and had been spending as much time with him as possible ever since.

When I went to New York that April on business, Nancy took my mother and me to the hospital with her to visit him. The last time I'd seen him, a year earlier, he'd looked much better than I'd thought he would, almost normal really, except for a tiredness around his eyes, a looseness in his muscles. But since then, he'd been hospitalized several times and had to stop working altogether, afflicted by AIDS-related pneumonia, a rare disease of the optic nerve, and finally a cryptococcal infection in his brain.

Now he looked far worse than I could have imagined: unbearably thin and pale, his face a bony mask, his hair shaved into a patch for surgery, all the curl gone out of it. The look in his eyes when he woke up and saw Nancy, the way he followed her every move, broke my heart.

Come give me a kiss, Nal, he said to her, in a scratchy whisper of his old New Jersey gangster voice.

When he noticed me and my mother, he smiled.

Mar, Jane. Thanks for coming.

We told him how happy we were to be there, tried to hug him around the tubes, gave him the flowers we had brought.

How's Tali? he asked me. Is he all right?

All right, I said. Not great.

Tell him to call me, said Steve. I want to talk to him.

He wants to talk to you too. Maybe he'll come up and visit, I said.

Nah, Steve said, he doesn't need to come all the way up here. I just want to hear his voice, know what I mean?

Yeah, I said, tears welling up, I know.

That night, we had dinner with my mom at an Italian place in North Jersey, then she drove home and I went back with Nancy to her apartment. Nancy and Steve's apartments had always been studies in minimalism. Steve's paintings on the walls, a shelf for the stereo and plants, maybe a fifties dinette set and a futon. The place was always clean, insanely so, I thought, thanks to Nancy's unique reaction to doing heroin. I'm serious, that girl would throw down her hypodermic needle and whip out the floor wax and the dust rags. I can remember being over there, all ready to go out, and Nancy would say, Wait, I'll be out in a sec. We stand there boiling in our coats until someone went to the bathroom to check and, sure enough, she'd be in there polishing the faucets.

When Steve and Nancy split up, of what little they'd had, she took nothing. For almost a year, she lived in an empty apartment, surrounded by encouraging greeting cards from friends in her twelve-step group. Gradually, she started buying things. She had a couch now, and Mexican candlesticks, a wrought-iron four-poster bed, even fluffy little rugs in the bathroom. The greeting cards were still on display; the walls remained clean and bare. Even without drugs, I noticed, she was still very neat.

The apartment looks great, Nan, I said, finishing my tour and joining her in the kitchen.

How's Tony, really, she asked, taking the Museum of Modern Art teakettle Steven had given her for her last birthday from the stove and pouring boiling water into two cups on her kitchen table. I figured maybe you didn't want to go into it in front of Mommy and Steve. Here, have some Sleepytime.

Oh God, Nancy, I don't know, I told her, stirring honey into the tea. His T cells are under a hundred, he's got thrush and diarrhea and bronchitis and night sweats and headaches and about a million different mysterious aches and pains. To say he's depressed is the understatement of the year. Not to mention fucked up on pills all the time.

And you? she asked.

Please, I said. I'm so stressed out I can barely breathe, and I know as bad as things are, they can only get worse. What's next? He starts getting sick like Steve and goes through a year of hell? He nods out in the car and drives into a tree?

Nancy followed me with her eyes as I got up and began to pace around her kitchen, my voice rising as I enumerated the possibilities on my fingers.

Or he ODs. He gets bad dope. He falls asleep with a cigarette and burns down the house. It's disgusting, but sometimes I feel like I'm just waiting for him to be gone so I can be a normal person again. I feel myself moving away from him, and that makes me sick too.

It's human nature, said Nancy wearily. It's easier to give something up before it's taken away from you. Even if you stay, you can't help leaving emotionally.

She yawned, pushed herself up from the table, and kissed me on the cheek. I'm exhausted, Mar, I gotta go to bed. I'll see you in the morning.

I went across the street to the Cumberland Farms to buy a

can of beer and drank it sitting on the front stoop of the garden apartment where my little sister lived alone. Then I went in and climbed in beside her in her new four-poster bed.

I couldn't read on the plane ride home. Steve's voice was in my head, that scratchy North Jersey hoodlum bass I loved so much, already almost silenced. I thought of his anger at Nancy, which had once seemed as bottomless as Tony's toward me, now somehow melted away. Could that happen for us before the eleventh hour, before the hospital rooms and funeral plans and goodbyes? At that moment, all I wanted was to somehow make Tony forgive me, for us to love each other as much as we could in the time we had left. Would there be no more happiness, no more fun vacations or private jokes or lazy Sunday mornings, no peace for us at all?

As I came down through the jetway into the terminal, I was thinking of a cartoon I'd seen on the front of one of the greeting cards in Nancy's living room. It showed the exit from the Tunnel of Love, the line of happy couples sailing along in their sweet little boats. Only to their surprise the tunnel stops short, the placid stream becomes a spillway, and they crash over the edge into a murky sea of flotsam and jetsam, smashed-up wood, and bewildered survivors treading water.

Then I saw my two little boys and their tall, skinny father waiting for me past the gate, and I swam over to them.

Steven died in the hospital a few weeks later. Tony and I got the news in the middle of Hayes's fifth birthday party. After I hung up the phone, we stood looking at each other for a second. I pulled him to me and felt the sobs shaking his tense shoulders. The cake, I mumbled after a minute, because Hayes had just blown out his candles and I was only coming in to get a knife. While I was out there supervising the opening of presents, the swimming, the helium-balloon poodles and swords, the distribution of favors and finding of shoes, Tony must have taken all the pills in the house, because by the time the party was over, he was so out of it, he barely seemed to hear me when I talked to him.

Just two days earlier, it had been Steve's thirty-sixth birthday, and Tony had called him in his hospital room. When he hung up, his face was hard and defiant, his eyebrows knitted together like his mother's. I'm not going through that, he said. It's bullshit. I'm not going to do it. Steve said he wishes he had blown his head off while he still had the chance.

But— I said.

But what? he demanded.

I don't know. I was just wondering what I would do. It must be hard to know when to give up fighting.

It's just like in a boxing match, said Tony, you stop fighting when you can't get up anymore.

Nancy and my mother went to the church for the funeral, but they were ostracized by Steve's family. The service was formal and impersonal, performed by a priest who had never met the deceased. Despite the stares she could feel boring into her back, Nancy stood a long time by Steve's coffin; she put a photograph of the four of us, all dressed up on the way to a Prince concert, next to his body. Afterward, nobody stopped to talk to her or even give them directions from the church to the cemetery, so by the time they got out there, it was almost over. They stood off to one side, the wind cold and straight in their faces, watching as the mourners each laid a long-stemmed red rose on the grave.

I sent those roses, Nancy told me on the phone, her voice more sad than angry. Can you believe that? They were my roses.

I found myself thinking, Roses—will Tony want roses? and then I went blank, leaping from my own train of thought like a hobo from a freight car, standing in a dead yellow field.

TONY IN THE GARDEN

He spends most afternoons in the backyard, bent over the flower beds, watering his hibiscus, his dahlias, his elephant ear, the new Lord Baltimore, picking bugs off leaves and petals, checking the progress of shoots and blossoms. The flowers are beautiful and orderly; they respond to the care they are given in predictable ways. Not like his children, a few feet across the yard, playing Throw All the Lawn Chairs into the Swimming Pool. The children are also beautiful, but chaotic and contrary. And not like his wife, who can be beautiful or ugly and who is at present holed up in Oregon at some women's writing workshop.

What a person can expect from a relationship with a plant is very limited, but in general, those expectations are met. He does not believe this to be true with people, though he doesn't often test the theory. It is best to rely on no one. Look, he relied on her, and she has betrayed him.

Let us count the ways:

She has had an affair with a twenty-three-year-old boy at work.

She has alluded to this affair in her stupid essays so everyone knows.

She has sent him to the supermarket, then criticized his purchases.

She has turned stingy in general.

She has stopped trying to get along with his mother.

She has shared his needles and borne his children and,
despite all that infected blood and semen, she is not
dying.

She will see his children grow up and he will not.

Her happiness is his sorrow and her sorrow is his sorrow and
he is sorry, she is sorry, they are sorry all the time.

His life takes place in a circumscribed space, its borders
marked as carefully as the school figures he used to trace in ice
with the blade of his skate, morning after morning, month after
month, all those years of his childhood.

Inside this tiny world, there are certain comforts: the flowers, the vegetables, the blue swimming pool, the pills that make
a warm space in his head. There are children, and there are coffee and cigarettes in the morning and videos and cigarettes at
night, and a great many cigarettes in between.

It is not enough, though, for a thirty-six-year-old person
whose time left may be measured in months. There has to be
something else, one last escape. A trip to Greece, maybe.

Greece? she replied, astonished. Not now, honey.

Not now? he shouted. When?

Something has been taken away from him, and he is not sure
who took it. It's not her fault, of course, nothing is her fault, so
it must be his. The seeds were germinating in his blood when she
met him, when she discovered him, when she came along and
took over his life and reinvented it ten years ago. Now everything is hers, and what is not yet hers will be when he is gone.
Even the flowers, but she will surely let them die.

Five P.M., any day of the week:

The back gate swings open, and she comes into the yard on
her bicycle in her cutoffs and sandals and tank top, her thick
brown bob.

Hello, she calls, coasting down the hill. She parks her bike and drops her backpack. How are you?

Fine, he says, smiling but unenthusiastic. How was work? he asks, meaning, Did you go down and smoke a cigarette with your little friend today?

Boring, she says, meaning, My job is not a romantic social occasion; it is the burden that I bear for you and the children. Are you sure you're okay? she says. You don't sound fine.

She is like this, very solicitous, always listening for signs of trouble.

I have a headache, he offers, to shut her up, give her her little codependent fix.

Did you take your pills?

Yes, I did.

Good.

But later he will be thick-tongued and heavy-lidded, and she will be angry because he took too many pills. It is hard to take exactly the right number of pills for her, and he does not even try. The pills, if nothing else, are his.

What about dinner? she asks.

I made beans and rice.

Great. Where are the boys?

Inside, watching "Ninja Turtles."

She goes in to greet them, a happy ritual. Mom-my! they cry in unison.

She has begged him, Please, let's just have this time together. Let's just be a family while we can. He would like to, no, would love to, but how is it possible with the fact of his death and her life slapping him in the face every minute?

There was a time when he had more power in this relationship, and the power was sex. She wanted him so badly.

She wore his clothes, she brought him drugs and bought him drinks, she filled sketch pads with drawings of him sleeping. She wrote down the stories he told her as if they were her own precious poems. She threatened to get a sex change. Finally, she threw herself around his room like a pillowslip in a tornado and smashed two chairs to bits when she saw him kissing an old boyfriend in a bar.

But he had never wanted a woman's body before, and hers was no different. What he wanted was her energy, her laughter, most of all, her love for him. Almost from the minute she walked into his life, she was like a radiant light source, an unflickering beam of approval and passion. Not just those first crazy months in New Orleans, it was years and years.

That's what the twenty-three-year-old jerk-off took away from him, and made him want her as he never had in his life.

The roses are not thriving, the ones he put in along the top of the blue-tiled retaining wall that runs along one side of the pool. He'd been worried about that wall—he could imagine the boys, a little older, catapulting disastrously from its four-foot height into the water, which is too shallow even at its deepest. He searched his nursery catalogs for the thorniest low-lying rose bushes, and planted them at intervals along the ledge. They would fill in and form a thicket, he thought, that the boys would learn to avoid after a single scratchy encounter. He could picture the pale yellow flowers above the indigo tile.

It has not gone as planned. The roses bloomed only once this year, early in spring, then never again. Now the green is seeping out of the leaves; some branches are already bare. He can't find the bugs, can't identify the fungus. The bristling hedge he imagined is a half-dozen spindly plants, chinked by great gaps of air.

Anyone could walk right over the edge.

LONG WAY DOWN

When I called home from the airport on the way back from the writing workshop in Oregon, Tony told me that Dr. Benito had diagnosed the sore spot that had appeared inside his mouth on his soft palate as a lesion caused by Kaposi's sarcoma. I heard the news with my body first, stomach sinking, throat closing, head pounding. Some people get KS and get over it—one friend of ours had some lesions ten years ago that went away; he had no other symptoms for all that time. However, with Tony's attitude and lifestyle, I saw little chance he would be in this group.

Though Benito had never been stingy with pain medication, the onset of KS overcame whatever resistance he had left to Tony's continual complaints about pain and requests for more and stronger medicine. The lesion itself was painful, and the chemotherapy treatments, injected directly into the roof of his mouth, leaving huge craters as they killed the cancer, were agonizing. Benito began to prescribe Dilaudid, then morphine, later a twenty-four-hour time-release synthetic-opium skin patch. Because of the steel-clamp addictiveness of these drugs, they are rarely prescribed in quantity to any but the soon-to-be-terminal, and perhaps those who drive their doctors crazy enough beforehand.

Within weeks, I found a spoon and a bag of syringes hidden in his salon, obviously for cooking up and shooting the little yellow Dilaudid tablets. I stared at those syringes, overwhelmed by loneliness. He was so far gone from me.

Night after night after night after night after night

after night after night after night after night after night after night after night after night after night after night his jaw sagged his eyelids drooped his hair hung his lip dropped the whole force of gravity dragged his sotted body and brain down down down. I felt as if I were watching his spirit, his personality, his life force, being suffocated, smothered, drugged into absence and submission. As if I were watching him die, or, sometimes, as if he were already dead, facedown in the dregs of his dinner.

The boys, having no concept of drugs or their effects, took it more or less in stride. Daddy's sleeping again, three-year-old Vincie would report to me. Shouldn't he take a nap in his bedroom?

Over the next few months, the cycle established with the Vicodin and Valium continued with these stronger drugs. Tony would take way more pills than he was supposed to, be blasted out of his mind until he ran out, then hit the wall and go into withdrawal, sweating puking shitting whining shaking not eating at all running fevers crawling out of his skin doing anything he could think of to get more. Since Benito refused to give refills before the next appointment, he would call our dentist, other people's dentists, doctors from the yellow pages, anyone.

Whether in pain, high, or in withdrawal, Tony was now out of commission most of the time. In addition to my job and my writing, I was taking on more and more of the housework and kidwork as well as dealing with his gnarly self. I was frazzled and exhausted and angry. As before, I would sometimes go find his pills and take a few myself. Though it would make things seem better for a couple of hours, in the end I would be not only more exhausted, but ashamed and confused.

Finally, I went with Tony to Benito to talk about the situation. The solution the three of us came up with was that I should hide the pills and dole them out according to the schedule. Though

Tony agreed to it, I was nervous about having any more power, any more reasons to be resented. We had so many things to fight about already. But there seemed to be no other choice.

I took my responsibility very seriously. I had a green-lined accountant's pad where I wrote down in columns how many pills I gave him at each interval every day; if he convinced me to pass out extras or if I took one myself, I wrote that down too. This worked for a little while.

In September, we went out to Liz's extravaganza birthday party—it was her thirtieth, her mother's sixtieth—at a hotel near Big Bend National Park in West Texas, a weekend-long event with a country-western dance band under the stars on Saturday night. We had all been looking forward to this party for almost a year. On the plane out, Tony seemed incredibly loaded, his lower lip loose, his eyes glazed, a sheen of sweat on his skin. I asked him if he had taken some extra pills, and he was infuriated with me for not trusting him. I couldn't believe he was so infuriated, which infuriated him further. The second we landed at the airport, he insisted he was going to get on a plane home and I fell right into the trap, begging him to stay, pleading for forgiveness. We went back and forth like that throughout the two-hour drive from the airport to the party, which was in progress when we arrived. He headed for our room; I went straight in to the party to say hello and have a beer or six.

When I staggered back to the room, I found him sitting on his suitcase on the porch, smoking and holding a drink, slumped over, slurry, groggy, eyes rolled up.

Where are you, Tony? Where are you? I asked him, slurring myself. This is not the you I know, not the real you.

Oh yes it is, he said.

No it is not.

Shut up.

Come on, I said, unpack. Stop being such a spoiled brat.

Go fuck yourself, he said, and elbowed me hard in the ribs and threw his drink in my face. Without even thinking, I beaned him with the beer bottle in my hand. Blood began pouring out of his forehead.

I ran inside to get some towels, frantic and guilt-stricken and too drunk to even think about being careful around all that HIV-rich blood.

The next day, the seesaw tipped briefly the other way. We drove into Big Bend with a couple of friends and spent the day in the middle of that vast nowhere, perhaps the richest, most breathtaking nowhere on earth. Our petty ugliness was no match for such raw beauty, the jagged terra-cotta cliffs against the fierce blue sky, desert plants and cactus blooming in the rock. We climbed to the top of a ridge and stood on a wide, flat boulder, looking out over the canyons and mountains. It was so clear, so sharp, so unforgiving and magnificent and vast beyond all sense of scale, as if we were taking a hike through the mind of God.

Tony had picked a prickly pear; he bit into the purple flesh, then passed it to me. It was sweet and astringent at once.

I'm so sorry I hit you, I said.

I was an asshole, he replied, I deserved it.

We should bring the kids out here sometime, I said. They would love it, don't you think? We could take the raft trip down the Rio Grande. We could camp.

You know how I feel about sleeping on the ground, Tony said. Let's get a room at the lodge. We should call right away, though; you have to make reservations way in advance.

And we continued to plan this vacation on the hike back to the car.

Our shaky peace held for the rest of the weekend, but I

couldn't stop going over in my mind how and why this had happened, just when things seemed to be going so well. Why did he
seem all junked out again when he was taking the same eight
pills a day that was the right dose the week before? I couldn't figure it out. Was it an alcohol interaction? Was he taking too much
of the Klonopin, a tranquilizer he was supposed to use at night
that I wasn't in charge of? He didn't have any money for street
drugs, at least I didn't think so.

When we got home, and I went to get the bottle I had hidden
with the following week's pills, I found out why. It was empty.
When I confronted him about it, he lied and lied and lied. For
days he kept it up.

Okay, if you didn't take them, who did? I asked. Hayes?
Vince? The next-door neighbors? Just tell me. Just give me one
reasonable explanation.

How dare you accuse me, he said thickly, when I'm trying so
hard?

This withdrawal was the worst one so far. He was immobile,
helpless, hopeless. By this time, I knew what to expect. Though
unsympathetic at first, soon I couldn't stand it anymore. I
dropped a letter off at Benito's office, describing in detail what it
was like for me, stuck in the house with two small children and a
raving maniac. You are complicit in this, I accused him, you have
to do something.

He didn't reply to my letter, or to the phone calls that followed,
which was not all that surprising since he had a waiting room full
of people, hospital rooms full of crises, and numerous patients on
their deathbeds every single day. Many months later, he showed me
the phone messages stapled into Tony's chart. Marion Winik called,
one said. Message: She cannot take it anymore.

Ray had scrawled in pencil, Who could?

The third day of that terrible withdrawal, angry at Benito's failure to return our phone calls, Tony stormed into the office without an appointment, demanding relief. They hooked him up to an IV, but when he found out it was only to rehydrate him, he ripped the needle out of his arm, jumped up from the table, and banged the door open, shouting and cursing and bleeding all over the place as he stomped down the hall and out of the office. Later that day, he calmed down; a doctor friend of ours had given him a prescription for Tylenol 4. He couldn't stand to see Tony suffer, and he agreed with him that, in this situation, there was no good reason not to stay high as much as possible. These rationales seemed reasonable if you didn't see the downside of the so-called relief.

The fourth day, Tony had an appointment with Benito and would ordinarily have gotten prescriptions for his refills. I had decided I could not let it happen. I couldn't stand the thought of him starting over when he had come this far, had already suffered what seemed to be the worst. I didn't want to see zombie-Tony again, didn't want to be with him, didn't want to inflict him on others. I wanted him to go away forever so the real Tony could come back.

I wept the whole time we were at Benito's office at our complete loss of dignity, both of us over the edge in our separate ways all week, at the horror of chemical enslavement, at what our life had become. Benito and I went back and forth as Tony sulked, answered questions in monosyllables. Benito wondered if he would like to try a new pain treatment for the sore in his mouth. A CAT scan would determine the exact source of the pain and a shot of ethanol would permanently kill the offending nerve. It was a state-of-the-art procedure; one of the experts was in our area.

Forget it, Tony said, I don't have time to wait in any more doctor's offices.

How can you say that? I demanded. This is something that could make your pain go away forever.

I don't believe it, he said. Is there a guarantee? I don't think so.

Well, it's worth a try, isn't it?

You kill one of *your* nerves, then let me know.

Don't you see, I exploded, turning to Ray, he's just sitting there waiting to see how long he has to sit here and bullshit with these two idiots before he can get his prescription, go down to the drugstore, and get these pills down his throat?

You get out of here, Tony said. Who invited you? Either you leave, or I leave.

That's enough, said Benito. Stop acting like a golden asshole. Don't you see you're about to lose both her and me?

Goddamn it, Tony wept, I'm finding another doctor. I don't see how this became her decision.

It's not her decision, it's my decision, said Benito. I'm not refilling the Dilaudid. I'll see you in two weeks.

That's it, Tony exploded, you're fired, Ray. And you—

He turned toward me with a look of pure hate.

I'll leave you two alone to talk, I said nervously, because I usually did this at the end of an appointment, and walked shakily out to the receptionist to pay. Tony flew out behind me, and I was so sure he was going to hurt me that I literally ran, raced down the back stairs to the parking lot, jumped in my car, and locked myself in. Tony came out seconds later, screaming and red-faced, and began pelting my car with packets of nonnarcotic pain reliever from the huge sample box Benito had just given him.

I started the engine, backed out, and drove away.

I spent the morning at the office, terrorized, making desperate phone calls to my therapist, his counselor, his caseworker at AIDS Services. Tony was coming in on the other line every five

minutes, threatening me, weeping, shouting, until I told the receptionist to stop putting him through. I was practically halluci-
nating from stress, feeling as if my muscles and organs were
gone and all that was left was brittle bones and the very next
thing that happened would snap me to pieces.

That afternoon I was supposed to bring a neighbor's child
home with Hayes from school, but the situation seemed too
volatile to have kids around. So I took them to the frozen-yogurt
store, to the park, to the grocery store. I let them each pick one
snack they really wanted me to buy, and that process lasted almost an hour. It wasn't that we couldn't narrow it down to
Lunchables, Squeezits, and Chips Ahoy; it was that they couldn't
agree on which belonged to whom.

So you'll share, I called, tagging behind them with the cart,
almost enjoying the reassuring normalcy of this pointless squab-
bling. Can't you share?

Yes, but they're mine, not his, said Vincie, clutching the
cookies.

No, you picked the Lunchables! Hayes retorted.

Did not! Daniel did!

Why does it matter, if you're all going to share?

Because they're mine!

Apparently, it was the principle of the thing.

Finally, we had to go home, but it was just as I suspected.
Tony was cursing, throwing things, stomping around, and I
could see the little neighbor boy hypnotized. My kids didn't pay
much attention at first, but then Tony smashed a Mexican bowl
of Mardi Gras beads a few feet away from where Vince was sitting coloring. Shortly after that, he ripped the phone out of the
wall and hid the cord, and I spent fifteen minutes searching for it
before I realized I better just get out of there. I scooped up the

children and took them down the street to play by the creek until I saw Tony's car leave the house.

The next day, he came by to say he was leaving town and he needed some money. I gave him checks to get a contact lens and a new tire and two hundred dollars in cash, and he left for New Orleans.

He apparently found a doctor to give him some pills and signed up for the city methadone program as well. Every time he called, he sounded blasted. Meanwhile, I was too busy to think; only after the kids were in bed, when I sat alone in the quiet house, Rocco purring on my lap while I flipped through a magazine, would I begin to brood.

But I *can* do this, I thought. A storm that week took down three huge branches from a tree in the backyard, and I sawed them up and hauled them away myself.

When he had worn out his welcome with all the people we knew in New Orleans, he came home, an emotional and physical wreck. Benito—he was unfired by this time—told me shortly after his return that Tony had six months to a year to live, though he had said that at least twice before.

He's got cancer of the attitude, Benito said. It's dragging him down fast.

Soon everything was worse than ever. He was taking acid, muscle relaxers, methadone, anything he could get his hands on, and was out till all hours almost every night. He told me he was sleeping in his car, but I soon found out he was staying with a guy named Jerry, who seemed to be something like a new boyfriend. He told me he was looking for an apartment.

I was so rocked by these developments that I could barely do much of anything except continually straighten up the house, controlling my little flock of objects since I couldn't seem to control anything else.

By December, Jerry was history and no apartment had been found. Christmastime brought with it a temporary reprieve, as Tony got busy with his seasonal rituals, fixing up the house, taking the boys to buy a tree, helping them hang ornaments and put up lights. He loved holidays; the storage area under our house was filled with boxes of decorations labeled in his handwriting: HALLOWEEN, MARDI GRAS, EASTER, THANKSGIVING, CHRISTMAS. I considered the holidays a huge chore, and I wondered all over again how I would ever manage any of this without him.

Christmas Eve we were up late wrapping presents and sharing a bottle of champagne along with the sandwich the kids had put out for Santa Claus. In the middle of our sweet parental ritual, he started asking me about a condom he had seen in my desk drawer. It isn't there anymore, he said. Where is it?

At first, I was frightened and I lied. Maybe the kids moved it, I said.

Oh, they did? Well, they conveniently stored it for you in your backpack.

Oh, shit, I thought, and then confessed that I had put it there.

He didn't say anything. I saw that he was crying. When I went over to put my arms around him, he angrily pushed me away.

I went in to check on the kids—they were sleeping together in the lower bunk, arms thrown around each other, dreaming, no doubt, about reindeer and elves and Mighty Morphin action figures—and came out with a strange resolve. I went straight to Tony on the couch and began to kiss and fondle him. At first, he brushed me off.

Why are you doing this, he wept, why are you doing this now?

But eventually he gave in and began to kiss me back and unbutton my shirt, putting that troublesome condom to good use then and there. And as we lay together afterward without moving, prolonging the closeness, I realized that what started out as a tactic or a bone to make him forget what a bitch he was married to had unexpectedly opened my heart. He got up and got us some cigarettes, and we stretched out beside each other, whispering and laughing and watching our smoke curl together in the air. We started to talk about the Christmas lights in Johnson City, whether it was too far to go out there with his mom and Rod when they came to visit, and somehow got in a debate over which was farther west, Johnson City or Marble Falls. I was sure it was Marble Falls and I asked him if he wanted to bet, and he did. I said whoever loses has to forgive the other for everything.

It was Marble Falls. For a few days, I was forgiven. If only we had found that magical way of bridging distance and dissolving tension more often. If only we could have been lovers all along.

THE LOVE CONNECTION

In February of 1994, I had to leave town for two ten-day trips to do publicity for my just-published book. By this time, it was clear that Tony could not be trusted to drive the kids around or be left alone with them. In addition to his basic zombieism, he had had several seizurelike episodes, each starting like an ordinary narcotic nod but followed by tremors, disorientation, and loss of coordination. One night, he was trying over and over again to shove a videotape into the audiocassette player. Another night at dinner, he was trying to pick up something with his fork and missed the plate completely, stabbing under the rim, then spent ten minutes in an attempt to cut a slice of cheese. Each time, I led him to the nearest couch, where he instantly fell asleep. Each time, when he woke up an hour or more later, he barely recalled the incident.

His short-term memory was falling apart as well. What are we having for dinner tonight? he would ask me, and I would tell him. A half hour later, he would ask me again. One time, half-joking, I wrote the answer on a Post-it note—LASAGNA—and stuck it on the mirror in his pink-walled salon, where he still spent a lot of time though he wasn't cutting much hair anymore. The note was still there the next day.

What's this piece of paper that says LASAGNA? he asked.

When we described these symptoms to Benito, he suspected that Tony might be beginning to suffer from AIDS encephalitis, popularly known as dementia. He ordered an MRI to see if there was anything identifiable happening to Tony's brain, but nothing showed up. But it didn't seem possible even to me that all of this was a side effect of drugs, the issue being whether it was "his fault" or not.

I asked Tony's parents and my mother to come down for two weeks each during my travels. Tony was planning to join me for the first part of the trip, at the events in New York and New Jersey, where he could see our old friends. And it was in New York, the night before he was supposed to return to Austin, that I came as close to killing another person as I ever have in my life.

After my reading at a café downtown, we were supposed to go out to dinner with a group of people to celebrate. We were all waiting outside the café, unfortunately situated on the Lower East Side, our old drug neighborhood, ready to get into the cars that would take us to the restaurant, when Tony said he was going to walk Steve's brother to the subway. We were all so surprised to see him there that night; he looked and talked so much like Steve, it was eerie. It was sweet of him to come, and walking him to the subway sounded like a nice thing to do.

So there I was on the curb with all these young writers and publishing people and my mother. It was very cold, and had even begun snowing lightly. Twenty minutes went by and Tony did not return. I insisted that we go ahead and leave.

Don't worry, I said. He'll find us at the restaurant. He knows where it is.

As we sat in the bar at the restaurant, having a drink before dinner, I could see that everyone was wondering where Tony was, starting to worry about how I might feel about having my husband mysteriously disappear on what was a pretty important night for me. I tried to assure them that it was no big deal. Let's just sit down and order, I said. He'll be back. He likes to eat.

Sure enough, as we were being seated, Tony reappeared.

Sorry it took me so long, he said briskly. I walked a little further than I meant to. I'll have a double vodka soda, he told the waiter, glancing over the menu, and the goat-cheese ravioli appetizer, and the steak. With a salad.

While we were waiting for the appetizers, my mother embarassing me with stories of my precocious childhood, Tony announced that he'd run out of cigarettes and had to go to the store.

No, look, Tone, I said, pointing to his pack of Newports, lying on the table with a few cigarettes in it.

But your mother's out of her Carltons and she's smoking all mine. I'll only be gone a minute, he said, and swept out the door.

Dinner was served, cleared, and utterly over before he came back. Most everyone had had to leave—the snow was now swirling thickly outside the restaurant windows—but I decided to stay a while and wait for him, unsure whether he knew the name of our hotel. As she put on her coat, my publicist gingerly expressed her concern about my disappearing husband.

Don't worry, he'll turn up, I told her.

She asked if there was anything she could do, and I confessed that I'd been wondering if it was possible to arrange for a car to pick him up at the hotel at seven the next morning. I was not confident that he would be willing or able to use public transportation to get to the airport on time. If he misses that plane, I'll die, I said.

She said it was no problem and kissed me goodbye. You better leave soon, she reminded me. You've got that radio thing with the station in Buffalo at midnight. "The Love Connection," remember?

I know, I said, I'll be there when they call.

Hard as it was to believe, I was scheduled to be the guest expert on a phone-in show about love problems.

The two friends who remained, Frank and Tina, said they'd help me find a cab; I asked the waiter to pack up Tony's untouched dinner. Just then, Tony returned, rushing to the table, disheveled and out of breath. He began pulling his necklaces and watch and money out of the front of his pants and dumping them on the table, while telling a confused and bizarre story about how he was almost mugged by a gang outside the convenience store where he went to buy the cigarettes. Frank and Tina were full of questions and sympathy. They ordered him a drink. I handed him the bag with his dinner in it and stared into space.

When we got back to the hotel, it turned out he had left his food in the cab. I had to go up to the room to wait for the call; he said he was going to stop in the bar.

I took off my clothes and got in bed. It had been a very long day of appearances and events, starting at 5 A.M., and I couldn't quite believe I had to talk to anyone about anything at that point. But promptly at midnight the telephone rang and we were on the air. The program consisted of people calling in to get my advice about their love lives. I talked to one woman who couldn't seem to get over the boyfriend who had dumped her, another involved with a man with an alcohol problem.

I know exactly how you feel, I said. I know it just seems hopeless, like you're spiraling down into this dark pit and you'll never get out of it.

Yes, yes! she said tearfully.

Well, I wish I knew something positive to say, but I haven't been out of the pit for a while myself, I told her, which started her crying, and then the host jumped in and cut to a canned commercial for their 900-number-meet-your-true-love service.

Please, Ms. Winik, she begged me while we were off the air, could you try to be a little more upbeat?

In the middle of the show, a waiter arrived with a second huge dinner Tony had apparently ordered. Shortly after, Tony staggered in. He sat at the desk, alternately eating his food and collapsing into it while I lay in bed praying for the show to end. Hardly anyone was calling anyway, since I had proven to be such a disappointing expert.

Finally, the hour was over and the argument that had been brewing all day began. Tony was in an insane rage, railing at me about everything I'd ever done to him and things I might do in the future, boiling over with fury and meanness. I put the pillows over my head, begging him to stop and let me get some sleep.

It was two in the morning. If I had had a gun, I definitely would have used it to shut him up.

He announced that he was leaving for the airport right then and there and started packing. I begged him not to. In his condition, I could just imagine what would happen to him out on the street. I figured I'd be hearing from the police within the half hour; I thought maybe I could call down and get the hotel doorman to stop him.

This proved to be unnecessary. He zipped up the huge suitcase, filled with free books from the publisher's office and the skin-care products he got me to buy him at Bergdorf's as a consolation for the fact that my agent and editor were buying me an outfit to wear on my tour as a publication present. (It wasn't enough, though. Later in the afternoon, he was standing in front of the mirror trying to wriggle his big arm into the sleeve, saying, I'm the one who's always wanted a jacket like this!) He heaved the suitcase with a groan and lurched toward the door. As he reached for the doorknob, he lost his balance, smacking his head and crumpling to the floor in a heap on top of his luggage.

Tony? I said, peeking out from under the pillow, but he was unconscious.

I thought about trying to move him, but I was too exhausted even to stand up, so left him lying there until the phone rang the next morning. Please tell Mr. Winik his car is here, said the voice on the other end.

Thank you. I certainly will, I replied.

This was easier said than done. After trying to wake him for a few minutes, I considered pushing him out the window. I imagined his body falling slowly through space, dropping spread-eagled and motionless on the gleaming black hood of the waiting car. Just then, he began to stir. He opened his eyes and peered around, completely disoriented.

Your car is here, honey, I said brightly. Have a great trip home. Give Hayes and Vincie a big kiss for me. Say hi to your parents. I'll call.

And I gave him a little peck on the cheek and pushed him out the door.

I called home the next day to make sure he'd gotten in all right.

He's at school, Grace told me.

What?

It's Thursday, you know, the day he volunteers at kindergarten.

Oh, I said, wow. I forgot. It had been surprising to me for a while that Tony had managed to keep up with this commitment, but never more than that day.

Once a week, Tony went to Hayes's school for an hour to help the teacher with small-group activities, folding his long body into a tiny green plastic chair at a low, circular table and playing alphabet card games or coloring with five or six kids at a time. Hayes was so proud—some other mothers came into class, but he had the only father that regularly volunteered. After the bell rang, Tony would eat lunch with Hayes and his friends in the cafeteria, opening milk cartons and passing out napkins, bringing a pocketful of quarters to buy them Popsicles.

Back in January, we'd gone with a group of friends to the local premiere screening of the movie *Philadelphia*. We got through most of it okay, but the hospital scenes were too much for either of us, and, sitting in the dark, we wept and wept. For us, it was no sentimental story, it was an instructional preview of the future, of the life-before-death that approached as surely as spring.

But now it was spring, and Tony was not in a hospital; it was time to put in the vegetable garden. He could still grow plants; he could still play Alphabet Lotto; most of the time, he could still cut hair. These simple acts of caring for other living things were the last places he was still himself, perhaps the last things tying him to this world.

MOVIE OF THE WEEK

Shortly after I got home from my book tour, I came to the long-resisted conclusion that Tony and I should not live together anymore. It took a whole Movie of the Week of betrayal, dysfunction, and violence, but finally I got the idea.

One Sunday evening in March, after I'd put the kids to bed, a friend called to ask me to meet him for a drink. Tony had been asleep for hours already, exhausted after whatever kept him out all night for the three nights preceding. Feeling that I deserved a little recreation, I decided to go, and woke Tony enough to tell him I was going out for a while.

The night lasted longer than I expected; after our drink, I went with my friend to his girlfriend's apartment for a nightcap. As I attempted to park my car at a gas station, across from her building, I backed over the concrete block that marked the end of the parking spot. My rear wheels were suspended in midair and I could move neither backward nor forward. We had to call the AAA.

By the time I bid my AAA rescuer adieu, it was midnight, but I had conceived the notion of stopping in to visit my friend Joe, with whom I hadn't had the chance to get together since I got back to town. When I called, he was already asleep, but he said to come by.

A local writer who worked for some of the same publications I did, Joe and I had met at a business lunch a few months earlier. He was a little older than I, recently divorced, with two children. We had met for lunch a few times since then, and I found his gentle, thoughtful demeanor very comforting. He was still very sad about his divorce, and the quiet, undramatic, unhysterical quality of that sorrow moved me.

That night, we looked at his slides of Mexico and France, drank wine, smoked cigarettes, and talked about my problems, of which there were many. As the hours passed, my glib facade began to crumble and I cried a long time in his arms. Something about him—his physical bigness, his calm solidity—made me feel safe, made me feel I could just let go. At 3 A.M. he gave me one last hug and I left reluctantly for home.

When I got there, Tony was awake on the couch, holding the alarm clock, electric with anger. I tried to cover for my lateness by telling him about the car getting stuck, but he was having none of it. He got up and slapped me, and I ran into our room but then came back to get the clock, worrying about getting up for Hayes in just a few hours. He wouldn't give it to me, but smacked me in the head with it, then pushed me by the shoulders to the wooden floor. I heard my head hit with a loud crack; I saw blood fly from my nose. I crawled away, but he came roaring after me and was dragging me down the hall by my arms and hair when suddenly we saw Hayes standing at the door of his bedroom, his face flushed with sleep, probably unsure if what he was seeing was real. Tony let go of me, and I ran to my son and slept on the couch with him in my arms.

In the morning, I woke up immobile, in pain and crying. I thought my tailbone might be broken from the fall to the floor. I called Benito, who said to come in right away, but I had to get the kids off to school first. Hayes asked if I was hurt because Daddy dragged me down the hall, and I made up some bullshit about grown-ups just playing a game.

A game? he asked. Then why were you crying?

Of course he didn't believe it. Just like Tony didn't believe whatever Grace had told him about the scenes he'd witnessed between his own parents when he was exactly Hayes's age. Among all the other feelings I had, I couldn't help thinking about how horrible Tony must feel about what Hayes had seen. He must have felt he was becoming his father, the person he hated most in the world, re-creating scenes he'd never dreamed he'd live through again, this time not as the terrified witness but as the towering monster. Tony's fatherhood was the only thing left in his life that he was proud of. All the gentleness and love, the hours of attention and care he had lavished on the boys— now these too were slipping from his grasp.

I spent an hour with Benito talking about what had happened, what to do. Looking grave, he said I was lucky not to be in the hospital with a head injury. He suggested family therapy, but that seemed like a Band-Aid for an amputation. I said I thought maybe I would have to get Tony to move out. He said he thought that was probably the best thing to do.

In any case, my tailbone wasn't broken, so I went in to work.

That afternoon, I called Tony's caseworker and told her what was going on. I told her how, once again, I was afraid to go into my own house. She said she'd been wanting to give me the number of an AIDS-aware divorce lawyer she'd heard good things about.

Divorce lawyer? I repeated. As soon as the word "divorce" came out of my mouth, what I had to do became crystal clear. For my children and myself, I had to break my promise.

That night, I told Tony I was finished with it. There's no turning back anymore, I said. I'm going to file for divorce tomorrow.

Well, then, he told me, I'm checking out. Don't try to stop me.

What do you mean?

I'm finished, too, he told me, unfolding himself from his hydraulic haircutting chair where he'd been sitting, as he did every night, chain-smoking. But I'm really finished, he continued, and got up and started to walk toward our bedroom, his face puffy from prednisone, his skinny legs sticking out of his cutoff overalls. Don't call anyone. Just leave me alone.

Are you saying you're going to commit suicide? I don't think that will be possible with me sitting right here, I called after him in an acid tone. If you want to commit suicide, you have to do it when nobody's home and nobody's expected for a while. And you certainly have to do it when your children aren't sleeping in their beds, about to be awakened in the middle of the night and traumatized for the rest of their lives. Tony? Please, Tony, listen to me. Don't do this now. Are you crazy?

By the time I got to the bedroom, he was swallowing handfuls of pills, Klonopin and Soma and I don't know what else. I was afraid to try to stop him physically, and unsure whether I should call EMS right away; I thought if they came while he was still conscious, he would try to fight them off. Should I wait until he calmed down so they could take him peacefully? Though I felt like I was thinking clearly, some faint alarm was going off in my head. I called a friend and asked what I should do.

For God's sake, Marion, call right now, he said. Right now.

I called EMS, then Benito, then our insurance company, ever mindful of that oxymoron about preauthorizing emergency treatment, and suddenly I had a fire truck and two ambulances and several police cars screaming and flashing in front of my door. I couldn't believe he was doing this with the kids around. My biggest concern, in this completely out-of-control situation, was that they not wake up. I stood out on the front porch as the troops poured into my house, begging them to turn their lights off and cut the sirens. Be quiet, I kept entreating them throughout the ordeal, my kids are sleeping. At any moment, I expected to see them shuffle out of their bedroom in their PJs, rubbing their eyes, as all those men in uniforms with blaring radios crowded around their unconscious daddy with tubes shoved up his nose and shirt cut open, poking him and shouting, Wake up, guy. Hey, dude. Wake up.

By some miracle, the children slept through the whole drama, even though they turned on the goddamn sirens again after they carted Tony out to the ambulance on a gurney. The next-door neighbors, a good-looking, healthy young couple whom I had mainly seen washing their car and walking their dog, came over to see what they could do.

Do you have anything to drink in your house? I asked.

They brought over a bottle of blush Zinfandel. This was not a suicide attempt, I said, more to myself than to them, it was a ridiculous, melodramatic gesture. An expensive, ridiculous, selfish, stupid, melodramatic gesture.

A cry for help, my neighbor suggested gently.

Maybe so, I mumbled. Maybe so.

If it was, it was certainly backfiring, making me absolutely determined to get him out of the house.

Lately, I have begun to think about what Tony must have felt when I told him I was going to file for divorce. With all that he had lost and was losing, he must have believed he would never lose me. I was the future to him; my love was the last support holding him up. When I think of this now, now that I no longer am so busy protecting myself and the children and justifying my actions, I can feel sympathy. My filing for divorce was the last straw, the end of whatever will to live he had left.

But at the time, I had to think of my own survival; it had really come to that. To Tony's anger and surprise, I met with the

lawyer the next day as scheduled. I set out in our temporary orders the most amicable provisions I could imagine. I would pay
him support, rent him an apartment, cover his medical bills. He
could come to the house and use the salon and see the kids as
much as he wanted, if he didn't threaten me, beat me, or harass
me. As long as he respected these conditions, I doubted I would
ever actually go through with the proceedings, and, as it turned
out, I never did.

I took the kids to the hospital to see him the next day. As we
drove across town, I tried to find a way to explain to them what
was going on.

You know how tired Daddy's been, I said, how he takes naps
all the time? Well, now he's so tired he has to go to a very quiet
place with lots of vitamins and rest totally.

But why? asked Vince.

I took a deep breath. He has something called AIDS. It's a
virus, a bad thing in your blood that makes your body very
weak, so you get other sicknesses, too. Bad sicknesses.

Can he get better from AIDS? Hayes wanted to know.

No, he can never get all better, I said, but he might get a little
bit better for a while.

God, said Hayes, all that medicine he takes and it doesn't do
a thing.

How did he get it? asked three-year-old Vince.

He got it from someone else who had it, I said. But it's very
hard to get, not like a cold or something. We don't have to worry
about getting it from him.

Who did he get it from? Vince wondered.

We don't know, honey.

I was a little worried about how to deal with this issue, and I
was also concerned that the question of whether he would die
might come up, but just then we passed a 7-Eleven and they

switched their line of questioning from how Daddy got AIDS to whether we could stop and have a Slurpee. Later that week, I heard them telling another kid in the pool that their dad had AIDS, and the little girl said her grandfather had it too. I decided to butt in and, after a few clarifying questions, had the opportunity to explain the difference between hearing aids and Daddy's AIDS. I could see I would be explaining things for a long time.

A few days later, Tony was transferred to an outpatient drug-treatment program and released. I insisted that he stay at the house that night.

I woke up at 2:30 A.M. to a sound like a dryer out of balance, only it was Tony's head hitting the bathroom wall in a terrible seizure. I went in and found him wedged sideways across the toilet, scared eyes looking out at me as he shook uncontrollably. I had never seen anything like it. I dragged him out of the bathroom and called the doctor, terrified. He said the seizure was probably caused by a too-abrupt change in his medication when he left the hospital, and that I should just bring him back in the morning.

All night, he kept me up with crazy delusions. Edie Sedgwick and her sister Kyra were in the house, he insisted, trying to steal my driver's license. Hadn't I read in the paper about their escape from the hospital?

There didn't seem to be any point in reminding him that Edie Sedgwick, the famous speed freak from Andy Warhol's Factory days, had been dead for twenty years, or that Kyra Sedgwick, a young Hollywood actress, was not her sister.

I was nervous about Tony moving out of the house in the wake of the seizure, but I was no longer willing to live with a violent junkie and the drug program didn't seem to be helping at all. One night, he went out to get a video and came back two and a half hours later and twenty-five dollars poorer. He told me some story about how he'd run into a friend and they'd gone for dessert and coffee.

For twenty-five dollars?

Oh, yeah, we also bought a carton of cigarettes.

You mean this carton, that already has three packs gone?

I couldn't stand the idiocy of this lie, and we argued bitterly. But the time had come to stop arguing, and just accept that his getting off drugs was a fantasy on my part. His addiction came first—no, first through fifth, just as it had with Nancy and Steven before him. It no longer mattered what I wanted, or even what he wanted—addiction was in charge. It would make all his decisions from here on out.

That weekend we went to a wedding. At first, I thought we were having another one of our magic days of reprieve. We both wept during the vows, each no doubt thinking how far behind us those promises were now, and afterward danced to Susanna Sharpe and the Samba Police, twirling around the dance floor in our party clothes, the ghosts of that beautiful fun couple we were once upon a time.

At the party afterward, Tony made a phone call, left "to buy some cigarettes" (isn't this the beginning of a joke? one I had already heard a few times?), came back an hour later and locked himself in the bathroom.

The next day, we were sitting out by the pool and he said he was going out "to buy new tubes for the kids at Toys 'R' Us." He came back after dark. He had to go to four different stores, he explained.

Fine, I said. Now I'm going out.

No you're not, he said. I'll leave the kids here by themselves.

Then you leave, I said. I've had it. You don't live here anymore.

He left for real that time, and never lived in our house again. He went to stay with our friends Liz and Margaret—they had recently moved back to Austin from Brooklyn—until he could find an apartment, by which time he had burned holes in all their furniture too.

That week, he missed Hayes's birthday dinner because he ran out a half hour before we were supposed to leave for the restaurant, purportedly to get a Coleman lantern for our camping trip with Hayes's friends the next day. I begged him not to go; I said we could get the lantern the next day. He showed up at the restaurant just as I was signing the charge slip with some story that he'd been waiting for us in the lobby for an hour and a half, and that before that his friend Whitney had dragged him around all over Austin but couldn't find the lantern. Of course, when we got home, Whitney was on the machine saying, Hey, Tone, I heard you were trying to get in touch with me. Give me a call.

The other messages for Tony were from people whose names I'd never heard before and whom he claimed not to know.

The action highlight of our Movie of the Week was a car chase. It happened when Tony stayed over at the house one night during Hayes's birthday weekend and searched my room and purse and found a letter I had started writing to Joe, who had been out of the country for several weeks. It had no salutation, but went on about how I missed him, how lonely the playground was without him. Before he left, we'd begun to meet regularly at a park after we picked up our kids at school, sitting on a bench talking while they played together. The letter said nothing overly mushy, but its intimate tone left little doubt that the intended recipient was more to me than just a friend.

Tony demanded to know who the letter was intended for,

and I wouldn't tell him. He started ripping pictures off the wall and tossed our wedding photo in the trash.

The next morning when I got to work, I realized the letter was gone. He'd gone back into my purse and taken it. I called him and demanded to know where it was. He said he'd thrown it in the garbage in the kitchen, which I'd taken out to the curb that morning. I drove home from work and picked through the whole bag twice. It wasn't there. I called him at Liz's house to ask him where it really was, and he insisted he was telling the truth.

I couldn't stand for him to have that letter, couldn't stand to see my relationship with Joe declared part of the war zone, didn't want Tony's battleships in my safe harbor.

Driving over to Liz's like a maniac, I saw her blue Bronco on the road going in the other direction, Liz driving and Tony in the passenger seat. I made a U-turn through the feeder lane of the highway and floored it, weaving in and out of traffic until I pulled up beside them. Liz turned off at a side street into a fancy residential neighborhood, and I screeched in behind her. I jumped out of the car and stood outside the passenger window screaming at him, blooming spring branches waving incongruously over my head. On a bench at the corner, a woman in a white maid's uniform sat waiting for the bus.

Where is the letter?

It's in the garbage, I told you.

It is not.

It is so.

Then go to the house and find it for me.

I don't go through people's garbage, he said contemptuously.

I'll stand here all day until you tell me the truth.

I don't have all day, Liz interjected.

See, Liz doesn't have all day, Tony told me smugly.

Finally, I had to give up. Poor Liz practically got her ear cut off when he trimmed her hair that afternoon, and my teeth hurt for days from the shouting and the stress.

Tuesday he was apologetic, so I decided to talk to him more openly, to tell him that the letter had been intended for Joe. By hiding the relationship, I was only giving weight to the view that there was something wrong with my having it. I didn't think so, so why commit the unnecessary crime of deception?

I knew that there was another decision I could have made—instead of deceiving Tony or telling Tony, I could have just postponed getting involved with Joe. Tony was dying, right? Why not just wait? What was so urgent? But at the time, "waiting" was not only a vague concept but a repugnant one. I had no idea how long Tony had left—months? years?—and certainly didn't want to be in the position of waiting impatiently for him to be gone. My need *was* urgent: I was emotionally starving. Our marriage had been virtually barren of warmth and intimacy for some time. Many of our friends had pulled away from us, some so angry at Tony for his more outrageous behavior that they wouldn't even come to the house. He had retreated from them as well. I was unwilling to further polarize the situation by lining them up on my side.

I had long since given up on being perfect, on conforming to the saintly ideal in my head of how I should behave in this situation. Partly Tony had pushed me to this, partly I had been self-indulgent, but in any case, I was way past martydom. I was beyond my limits, drowning, feeling the tentacles of the same self-destructive impulses that had Tony so firmly in their grip. I needed a rock to cling to. Joe was a rock. Perhaps his being there for me would enable me to go on being there for everyone else.

I called Tony and invited him out to lunch. He said sure, and asked me to pick him up at his new apartment.

I sat on the bed in the little studio, looking around as I waited for him to get dressed. He had of course managed to make the place attractive, though a number of bounced checks and unpaid credit-card bills had accumulated in the process. There were his Virgin of Guadalupe pictures on the wall, his Day of the Dead figurines and candles and plants, the children's finger paintings and get-well cards taped to the refrigerator. He had a CD player, a TV, a vintage club chair, a fifties dinette, a matched set of floor lamps spray-painted antique gold. The apartment was located right behind the movie-rental store, which led the children to tell people that their father was living at Blockbuster Video.

You know that guy Joe? The writer? I began. Well, I've been spending time with him over the past few months—I like him a lot.

He looked blank for a minute. Then he realized who I was talking about. Joe? he said incredulously. Eeeww, gross. How could you be interested in that doughy lump?

This made me laugh. I think he's cute, I said.

Tony was standing at the closet, shirtless, trying to find something to wear to lunch. Have you seen this shirt Liz gave me? It didn't fit her, but if I wear the sleeves rolled up, it's fine on me. He put on a soft olive button-down shirt with tiny black dots woven into the fabric. It's Matsuda, he told me.

Let's go, Mr. Fashion Plate.

Over our spinach enchiladas, I wondered aloud if he had any romantic prospects on the horizon. What about that little guy at the pharmacy? Every time I go in there, he asks about you.

He does? Well, I spend enough time in there, waiting for re-fills.

Yeah, he's a little on the slow side. One might even say dumb.

He said, So what. I want someone dumb.

I laughed. That's perfect, I said. You want dumb, I want fat.

When I got home from lunch, there was a letter from the bank saying I should come in immediately and deposit $999,744.26 to cover my recent withdrawals. I reread this astonishing sentence several times. Even for the Movie of the Week, this was over the top.

I arrived at the bank shortly thereafter sans the requested million. It turned out the figure was a computer error, but they had in fact frozen my account because I was so overdrawn. Not until they showed me a printout of the withdrawals did I realize that Tony had been taking money again. I stared at the figures on the green bar paper, sixties and hundreds, almost every other day. Because his name was still on the account, he could go into any branch and get money, even though he didn't have checks or an ATM card anymore.

I managed to fill out the papers to close the account and open a new one before I went into hysterics, but the bank officer had to come out from behind his desk and try to calm me down.

Soon after this, Tony began borrowing money from all our friends, fifty bucks at a time. I called him and begged him to stop. Do you really want to do this? Do you want to be this kind of person?

I had always known that if I made him move out, he would go downhill fast, and it was this knowledge that made me resist for so long. I was certainly right: from the day he left home, his decline picked up momentum at a frightening pace. I had to keep telling myself I'd made the right decision, the only sane decision. I had to think of the kids and of myself, I had to get us out of the path of the runaway train Tony had become.

I had to let go.

BROKEN ANIMALS

In mid-May, I was scheduled to do a reading at a local coffee-house with the other members of my writers' group. The day of the event, I found an anonymous note in an unfamiliar handwriting stuck in my mailbox. It asked if I would read a poem from my first book, an obscure small-press volume published fifteen years earlier. I was touched by this request (actually, it made me feel sort of famous) and took the book along with me.

Tony showed up at the reading that night, looking truly like an AIDS victim for the first time. He was gaunt, his eyes cloudy, his cheeks sunken, and his movements awkward; he had recently been diagnosed with an infection called mycobacteriosis, or MAI, which caused swelling of the liver and spleen and serious abdominal pain. Benito wanted to admit him to the hospital for an aggressive IV antibiotic treatment to begin the following week.

Up to that point, except for the KS lesion in his mouth and a few brushes with what might have been pneumocystis pneumonia but had cleared up before an unequivocal diagnosis could be made, Tony had never had one of the defining illnesses of AIDS. The effects of the disease had been gradual and hard to pin down, complicated by the narcotics, the side effects of other medications he took, and his mental and emotional state. In some strange way, his finally falling prey to a major AIDS-related illness was a relief. He had been ready for some time to be an invalid—his self-incurred hospitalization earlier that spring was some indication of his desire to get the show on the road—and now there was no doubt that he was one. He would move very quickly to being ready to die. Again, his mind would beat his body to the punch.

In light of the pain of MAI, Benito had given him a new pre-scription for morphine—at least this kept him off street dope—and he was very high the night of the reading. He sat at a table outside the café most of the evening; I could see him through the window. He was all angles, neck bent, head dropped to the side as if on a broken spring, slack chin jutting almost into his chest, elbow propped on the table, hand dangling from his wrist. Only the cigarette between his fingers was not subdued by gravity, a stick of chalk floating above it all, smoke drifting up into the lights.

At the end of my reading, I told the audience about the note I had received that day, and read the poem. I noticed Tony in the back of the room crying when I read it, and, looking at him, I al-most didn't get through it myself, especially the last lines: *Love your old mistakes like broken, helpless animals / and they will heal / and they will lead you home.*

After the performance, I stood with Tony on the sidewalk. He was telling me about the MAI, and then confessed that it was he who had made the request for the poem; he had had Margaret write out the note for him so I wouldn't recognize the handwrit-ing. I wrapped my arms around his bony frame and held him for a long time.

The next day, I took Tony over to the hospital to check it out. The difference between this place and the facility he had been in in the wake of his suicide attempt was heartening. The atmo-sphere was comfortable and accommodating, the people com-passionate. The rooms were spacious and sunny, each with a wall of windows and a door to the lush inner courtyard, a VCR, a re-frigerator, and a sleep sofa for overnight guests. By the time we finished our tour, Tony seemed ready to move in. They said they would have a bed for him the next day.

I told him I would pick him up and drive him over.

No, I'll just drive myself, he said.

Are you sure? Honey, you really shouldn't be driving.

I could shoot a gram of dope, go blind, have a leg amputated, and still drive better than you do, Tony retorted, his old self again.

The boys were out of school and about to start a half-day camp program at one of the city recreation centers. The next evening, I took them shopping for shorts and sneakers, and we had tacos in the food court at the mall.

Daddy's in the hospital again, I said. Not the same hospital. A much better one, with a VCR and a fridge in his room, and a beautiful fountain outside. Let's buy him a box of candy and go over to see it when we finish dinner.

Is Daddy going to die? Hayes asked me immediately, his gaze meeting mine straight on.

He might, I said gently, laying my hand over his on the table, knowing the time had come for me to acknowledge this.

What will Daddy wear in the hospital? Vincie asked. Will he wear a blue nightgown with no buttons?

No, I think he'll wear his regular clothes this time. His T-shirts.

Where would he put his T-shirts? Vincie continued.

There's a little cabinet for his clothes. You'll see. Come on, let's go.

We spent the evening with Tony, who seemed very weak, as if the nervous tension that had been keeping him going had left him. The kids insisted he get up so they could play with the controls on his hospital bed, and I told them no, but he said it was fine and moved to the couch.

The staff of the hospital was even more impressive than the physical environment. Within the first few days, it was clear to me that Tony was being cared for in the most loving way imaginable. His main nurse, Mary Caldwell, was a slim, vibrant woman with gray hair, cornflower blue eyes, and a long history with the Quakers in various political-resistance and refugee movements. She seemed to take a special interest in Tony, and he adored her.

As if there weren't enough major life changes going on at once, I quit my job of almost eleven years the week Tony was admitted. Actually, I took a six-week unpaid leave, but I had serious doubts that I would go back at the end of it. With the kids out of school for the summer and Tony so ill, I literally had no time for work anymore. I thought maybe when things calmed down, I could support us with my writing. If that didn't pan out, I would get another job. Whatever. Long-term planning was not a big issue for me at the time.

Benito had thought the antibiotic treatment would take eight to ten days; as it turned out, Tony was in for almost three weeks because the high doses of antibiotics resulted in additional liver problems. We had planned to drive up north in June to Tony's mom's place in the Poconos. Tony and the kids were supposed to stay with his family while I spent a week at a writers' retreat, then came back to pick them up, stop in at my mom's, and drive home.

By the time Tony was discharged, we were supposed to be leaving in a few days, but Benito was extremely doubtful about the plan. Tony was in some degree of pain almost all the time, dependent on massive amounts of morphine. He weighed 125 pounds, 15 less than his normal weight. The MAI was not cured; pneumonia continued to threaten.

But he was determined to go. The trip was his last chance to spend some time with his mother and the rest of his family, my

mom and Nancy, Sandye, Pete and Shelley. His mother in particular had the need to do something, to take care of him, and I
knew it would make things a little easier for her if she had that
chance. Tony was very strongly against having people come
down to Austin—the idea exhausted him, I think, because he
kept imagining these visitors would be like houseguests he
would have to take care of and entertain—so going up north
was the only way these last meetings could occur. It would also
give him a way to spend some time with the boys in this place
which had been such a big part of his childhood.

So we went. We flew instead of driving, we shortened the
trip by a week, but we pulled it off. Benito had given me a letter
to show to other doctors listing his medications—there were
over a dozen by this time—and explaining that Tony was "terminal in the near future." We were to use this if problems came up
or if he needed refills on any of his drugs. When we got to his
mother's, having spent a few days with friends in western Pennsylvania, I gave her the letter, saying she would need to start calling drugstores right away. He was already out of morphine; he
had gone through a hundred pills in the first four days. I had only
been able to get him the liquid kind while at our friends' house,
which he was not happy about because it couldn't be cooked up
and injected, but now the bottle was almost empty anyway.

The next day, I left for Georgia in Grace's car, glad someone
else was in charge for a while.

While I was away, Shelley and Pete drove down from the
Adirondacks to see him; he could hardly get out of bed to sit
with them for a while. When I called, he was often asleep, so I
talked to Grace, to the boys. They sounded good. To them, it was
summer vacation in the mountains. They were sleeping in a tent
with Huey, Dewey, and Louie, seeing fireworks, eating Grand-
mom's cooking. One morning, Tony felt well enough to take

them out in the boat and show them the scruffy little islands where he used to fool around as a boy. They still talk about this a lot, how while they were having their picnic the boat drifted away and Daddy had to wade out in the water and get it back. Daddy was great! Hayes says. He saved Grandpop's boat!

That one stolen hour, the last time he ever really played with them.

It was awe-sun, says Vincie, mispronouncing their favorite adjective as he always does. Even he let me drive!

SISTER MORPHINE

He's stopped taking everything except the morphine, Grace told me after I got back from my retreat in the woods.

Yeah, he told me on the phone.

He doesn't see any point, he just wants to hurry up and get it over with now, she said, stirring blueberries with sugar in a bowl. He's never going to be able to travel or play with his children or do anything he wants to do ever again. The medicine is just prolonging his misery. He remembers what Steve went through at the end and he says he's not going to do it.

What do you think about that? I asked.

I don't want him to suffer anymore, she said. Whatever he wants, I want.

She gave me Benito's letter, quite dog-eared by now, along with a plastic pillbox and a small notepad filled with dates and tallies. She was holding the pills and doling them out on a schedule, as I once had.

You had to take the pills away from him? I said.

Yes, she said, he ran out twice. We had to drive all over the state to get the refills, and you should have seen the bottle one pharmacist pulled out. It must have been there for thirty years. Anyway, I don't think there is any more morphine in a two-hundred-mile radius of here, so I couldn't let him run out again. There's enough here to get you home, if you follow the schedule. You shouldn't have to get any more while you're at your mother's.

Okay, I said, thanks. I looked over the neat pages of numbers.

Some days he asked for extra and I gave it to him, she said. But if you keep doing that, you won't make it till the end of the trip.

I smiled ruefully; this story was so familiar to me. Is there something I can do to help you with dinner? I said.

Oh, no, she said. Just relax.

I picked up a packet of photos and began to flip through them. They were from a previous summer's visit; the boys were smaller, Tony nowhere near as thin. Do you remember the first time I came here? I asked Grace.

How could I forget?

You hated me, didn't you?

No, she said, not at all. We thought you were really weird, but perfect for Tony. We could never imagine what kind of person he would end up with, and when we saw you, we said, Yeah, this is it. She's perfect for him.

I could hardly believe what I was hearing; tears filled my eyes. I'm so sorry about everything that's happened, Grace, I said.

I'm not, she told me, in her usual feisty tone. I think meeting you and having those boys added years to Tony's life. I think he was on his way out back in New Orleans when he first met you, and all of this has been like a bonus. It's a miracle, about these boys. How many guys with AIDS get to have children, get to enjoy those babies the way Tony did?

By now, tears were pouring down my face, and Grace slid a box of tissues toward me. Outside, I could hear the voices of the children running toward the house—Uncle Sam caught a fish!

I can't believe we're having this conversation, I sniffled.

Well, we had it, she said briskly. Now we don't have to talk about it anymore. Go down to the dock, would you, and tell everybody to come in for dinner.

A couple of times that last summer, I did morphine with Tony, as if getting high together would somehow close the gap between us. It was one of the oldest rituals of our relationship, but everything had changed. For Tony, shooting up was mechanical now, not social or fun. And for me, not having shot up in so long, it was a disaster. The first time, I had a terrible reaction, throwing up and running a fever all night long, almost too sick to move. The second time was better, but it was still a mistake, producing neither the intimacy nor the relief I craved, and sending Tony a very mixed message. Every time I saw the track mark on my arm, I felt ill all over again.

Soon these drugs will be out of my face, I thought, and I will be all right.

After the trip up north, Tony was a wreck. Out of morphine again—the bottle of pills had disappeared while we were at my mother's house, he said I had misplaced it, I thought he had stolen it, and we fought bitterly over this in between my frantic calls to doctors and trips to pharmacies—he went straight back to the hospital from the airport.

You don't want to go home? I asked him.

I don't have a home, he said.

You could come back to our house, I said hesitantly.

No, it'll never work. Being around the boys exhausts me. I don't even want them to see me like this anymore. And you have a lot going on. I'll just get in your way.

No you won't, I protested, but I suppose I was glad he insisted on going to the hospital.

I'm ready, Tony told Benito the minute he walked through the door on rounds the next day. I want this over.

Ray wasn't surprised. Tony had talked about suicide before.

Ray and I sat in the courtyard of the hospital and discussed the situation. He told me that, given that Tony was suffering from three potentially terminal diseases—AIDS, drug addiction, and clinical depression—his impulse to end his life was not unexpected. What lay ahead was only more pain and debilitation, humiliations like diapers, which we both knew would be worse than death to him. He has no more than a few months anyway, he said.

That's what you always say, Ray, I told him, but I began to think about the phrase "complications of AIDS," so often cited in obituaries, and to consider Tony's particular group of complications. It was complicated to live almost ten years with a terminal illness. It was complicated to have diarrhea and headaches and night sweats almost every day of his life, lesions in his mouth, chronic pain. It was complicated to be completely reliant on narcotics for relief of both this pain and the even bigger one in his heart. It was complicated to decide that the future held nothing for him but further anguish, more drugs, and new afflictions, to feel that he no longer had the energy to be with his children. These, as well as chronic pneumonia and Kaposi's sarcoma and mycobacteriosis, all of which he now suffered from, were Tony's complications. I could understand his urge to escape them.

If I was willing, there was a way I could help Tony do it, the fastest, most painless, and foolproof way, with a lethal injection. My initial reaction when Tony asked me if I would do this for him was yes, of course. Who but me, closest to him of anyone, should help?

We celebrated Tony's thirty-seventh birthday and Vincie's fourth on July 19, 1994. Tony came home from the hospital to make an appearance at Vincie's pool party, but the merry chaos was too much for him. Just coming to the house, which he hadn't seen in a couple of months, was overwhelming in itself. His eyes dark and wet under the rim of his too-big black straw hat, he kissed Vincie and asked to be taken back to the hospital after less than an hour.

That night, our closest friends gathered in his room at the hospital, bringing in food and music and bottles of Taittinger. I was wearing a dress I had bought in the French Quarter the year we met, and our photo albums were lying around for people to look at. We had gone through them together the day before, laughing and crying over everything we had been through. We agreed that our marriage was the best stupid mistake we had ever made.

Tony's birthday party involved a great deal more dancing and smoking and drinking than most hospital-based celebrations. I feel like I'm getting to come to my own wake, he exclaimed. This is great.

Right after his birthday, Tony became absorbed in getting ready to die. He wrote letters and postcards to his mother, step-father, brothers, other family and friends. From his collections of folk art and jewelry and CDs, he selected gifts for people. He had asked his mother for a cedar chest for his birthday; she had shipped one down. Now he packed it with keepsakes for Hayes and Vince. He showed me the items he had selected: his favorite sweaters and necklaces, his ice skates, his haircutting scissors, his collection of pictures of the Virgin of Guadalupe. He put in some of the drawings and get-well cards they had made for him, as well as an old clipping from the *New York Times* comparing Madonna and Judy Garland. He wrote each of them a long letter and made them an audiotape so they wouldn't forget his voice.

He asked me to get rid of his apartment; he transferred the title of his car to my name. He gave me instructions about his memorial service and his cremation. Get two urns, he said, one for my ashes and one for Peewee's. Put us next to each other.

Peewee's ashes were still sitting in the plastic box in which they had been returned to us, just as my father's ashes had been some years ago when they were stolen by a robber from my mother's bedroom in New Jersey. The creep must have thought it was a jewelry box when he swept it off the top of her dresser along with her valuables and mementos. We got great pleasure from imagining the look on his face when he finally pried the tightly sealed container open. Talk about bad karma.

Tony gave me two *milagros,* Mexican amulets, to hang on his and Peewee's urns. Here, he said, this is the security system.

As Tony made his plans and preparations, I began to struggle with my decision to help him. For one thing, from my point of view, his physical condition did not seem that dire. He was not in agony, was not on his deathbed. Wasn't he rushing things? Was it really time? But finally I asked myself how much he would have to suffer to convince *me* that it was enough. And even if his physical condition was not yet extreme, his mental lapses, due to dementia or morphine or both, were becoming more frequent. One night on the phone out of nowhere he asked, Have you seen the steamboats? The water in the ocean is so much warmer now.

There is no ocean for hundreds of miles from Austin. I began to see that if Tony did not make his choice, he could lose the capacity to choose. Then what would I do? Go to the hospital, shoot him with a rifle, and tell the police that's what he wanted?

Sometimes, we were so close and it seemed we had let go of all the bullshit between us. Several times he asked me to stay over in the hospital with him and we held each other all night in the narrow hospital bed. A couple times, the boys stayed too, a little slumber party. They loved it when the orderly brought our breakfast in the morning on a tray.

But more often, I still felt anger and resentment, power struggles and manipulation. I saw him putting me in control of his death as he had so much in his life. If things were not completely clear and loving between us, if this bitterness was still there, how could I possibly be involved in helping him die? Wasn't his wanting me to help him die a way of making me take over, do it for him or to him, be responsible for this act as I was supposed to be for everything else? Marion, source of good and evil, Marion source of life and death. You ruined my life, you bitch, now finish me off.

Of course, I knew there were also legal issues, but they seemed irrelevant compared to the moral and emotional ones.

I asked our friend Clay, a counselor with years of AIDS experience, to come to the hospital and help us talk it out. Tony was irritable from the outset, not understanding why all this talk was necessary. When he realized I was considering reneging on my pledge to help him, his anger mounted. At one point, Clay asked me what I wanted from Tony that would make me feel okay about being involved with his suicide. I said that I guessed I just wanted to know that when all was said and done I had his blessing to go on with my life, that he wished me well.

Don't be ridiculous, Tony sputtered. You've already gone on with your life. You never needed my blessing before.

I felt as if I'd been slapped. I'm not asking your blessing on my future orgasms, Tony, I said.

You're disgusting, he said.

Tony, you're leaving this woman to raise your children and preserve your memory, Clay said. It's a passing of the torch she's looking for, a recognition of what lies ahead of her.

I was in tears by then, saying over and over to myself, He does not wish me well. He does not wish me well.

And somehow he did not realize this meant I was not going to give him a lethal injection, or else he forgot that it happened, because we had to have the whole discussion all over again, twice.

Even though I didn't want to give him the shot myself, I was still willing to help him find and carry out another course of action, as long as it didn't involve my assuming total responsibility. We both read Derek Humphry's *Final Exit* and Jessamyn West's *The Woman Said Yes* and discussed the alternatives. The possibilities seemed to be that Tony could either just refuse food and water, he could suffocate himself with a plastic bag, or he could overdose on sleeping pills. As was no surprise, he was not into the no-food-and-water idea, and the plastic bag sounded grisly to me, so Nembutal was the solution.

I agreed that he could come to the house and I would stay with him while he did it, and he made me a list of supplies I was supposed to get together.

By this time, I had started to feel like I'd gone through the looking glass, past the fourth dimension, into a situation more bizarre than any I had ever known. The whole sequence of events—agreeing to give him the lethal injection, becoming leery, then backing out after the session with Clay, helping him research alternate methods, finally shopping for the big event itself—was surreal. I felt like I was going to faint as I drove around and collected the items—prescriptions, wine, candles, a certain brand of strawberry-banana yogurt to smooth the digestion of the drugs—paid the smiling cashiers, and took my change. The kids were with me. I bought them candy bars at the pharmacy. In the wine store, the clerk was asking me, Is this for a birthday? A special occasion? It was all I could do not to break down.

Tony had arranged for Benito to discharge him from the hospital on the day he planned to kill himself. I was supposed to bring the kids over to say goodbye, then take them to a friend's house, come back and get him, and bring him home. But too many people at the hospital had put two and two together. While some of the staff were sympathetic with Tony's decision, they could not support euthanasia. And some had decided they were not going to sit still for it.

As I drove up with the children, having told them that we were going to give Daddy a big hug because he was probably going to die soon, I saw Benito sitting there with Tony in the courtyard. Benito never came to the hospital in the middle of the day, because he had office hours, so I knew something had gone wrong.

It turned out he was telling Tony he couldn't discharge him, that the hospital staff was in an uproar, someone had threatened to call the district attorney. He asked Tony as a personal favor not to kill himself.

Tony was furious. He was totally ready, poised like a diver, every spiritual muscle tensed; to be told to come down off the diving board was just too much. But he had no choice. He was so upset, he didn't even let me bring the kids inside. I turned

around and went home as ordered, shell-shocked. I kept thinking of the expression "stark staring mad" and feeling stark, staring, and quite mad as I sat in the house I had spent six hours
cleaning and fielded premature sympathy calls from family and
friends who knew of the plan. It was all I could do not to unplug
the phone. Sandye was already on her way down to help me after
what was supposed to be his death. It was too late for her to
change her ticket and I was glad.

For the next few days, Tony was like a hostage at the hospital,
stewing and suspicious of everyone. Somehow his being
thwarted by busybody outsiders put me more solidly in his
camp, made it a political issue rather than a personal one. I was
angry that laws and medical ethics prevented even those who
supported his decision from helping him, and became determined to help him overcome the obstacles. He had gone far
enough on his own. All the strength I ever gave or loaned him,
why would I refuse it now? After calling a lawyer, I offered to
bust him out and drive him to Louisiana, where the Texas D.A.
would not have jurisdiction. But he was going on about the
steamboats again, and our friend Clay, the one person I felt comfortable asking for advice, had left for a month's vacation. I had
no idea what would happen.

My mother, who knew everything, called to send Tony her
love and to tell him she knew he was trouble from the minute I
bought him that suit, making her that day's winner in our ongoing gallows humor contest.

Tony had a hard time being direct with his own mother and
also was *non compos mentis* much of the time, so Grace was rely-
ing on me for updates. We talked every day. I swore to her that
if the time came, I would make sure she had a chance to say
goodbye.

Four days after the false alarm, on Saturday, August 20, 1994,

Tony called and said he'd decided this was it. No one knew, so no one could try to stop him. What did I think?

It's your call, honey, I said. Tell me what to do and I'll do it.

We decided not to put the kids through a goodbye scene, especially after the botched attempt on Tuesday. They'd been over Friday to visit and though they rarely talked about death with him as they did with me, he told me that Hayes had asked him what an angel looks like, if they really have wings, and are they really naked? I'd gone out to run some errands, and when I came back found them cuddled on either side of him in the narrow bed, all three of them napping, and I knew there was no better last memory than that.

At one o'clock on Saturday, Sandye and I picked him up from the hospital. He seemed more relaxed and together than he had in months. Dressed in his platinum silk jacket with matching shorts, he asked me to take him to the Four Seasons hotel for lunch. We sat at a bay window overlooking Town Lake, and ordered Bloody Marys.

Good, Tony judged, after a sip, but not as good as mine.

He also had a spinach omelette and a piece of peach pie with ice cream for dessert. After lunch, he had me take him over to Liz and Margaret's, where he spent the afternoon telling them what they should plant in their garden, while I cleaned the house again.

The kids had been playing at their friend's house down the block; when I called, Daniel's mom said it would be fine if they spent the night. Send them home for their things, I told her, and they were at the front door two minutes later, panting with excitement. We get to sleep over Daniel's! Vince informed me.

She knows that, Hayes told him.

Here you go, I said, handing each one his backpack. Don't

forget to brush your teeth. Be good for Tomi and Dan. I'll see you in the morning.

I stood on the porch watching as they marched down the street with their packs on their backs like brave little soldiers.

At 6 P.M., Margaret brought Tony home for the last time. He went into the bedroom and changed out of his suit into a T-shirt and cutoffs. I had set our wedding photo on the night-table beside the bed; he tucked that postcard of the dancer into the frame and surrounded it with candles. He took his six o'clock shots of morphine and Valium—he had been very insistent on not missing them—and then an antinausea medication.

His mother called at 6:30, as I had suggested, and they talked for a few minutes. He cried only a little. After all the crying he had done in the past few years, he hardly cried at all that day, but he seemed more himself than he had in a long time.

Thirty minutes after he'd taken the antinausea medication, I handed him a bowl of strawberry-banana yogurt into which I had dumped the contents of sixty capsules of Nembutal, according to Tony's instructions. I took one taste of the concoction with my finger—it was horrible. He's never going to eat this, I thought.

It tastes like shit, I told him.

Put some jelly or something in it, Mar, he said.

I put in about half a jar of jam and several spoons of sugar. It still tasted awful, but he downed it in seconds.

He wandered outside to sit by the pool, smoke a cigarette, and drink a glass of wine. I followed him, but was too antsy to sit down. Look, Tony, I said, picking up the garden hose, I'm watering your flowers. They're doing pretty good, don't you think?

About two plants later, I saw the sleepiness come over him. I dropped the hose and helped him into the bedroom. I lit candles and crawled into bed beside him. I kept trying to talk to him— stupid questions like how do you feel? are you all right? do you want me to do anything?—but he was already too sleepy to answer. I touched his face, his body, smoothed his hair.

Then just before he fell asleep, he took the diamond earring I had put in his ear the night I pierced it in New Orleans so many years before out of his ear and gave it to me.

You wear this now, he said.

At 7:20 that evening, my excitable boy, my husband Tony, died beside me in our bed, the same bed in which Vince had been born on Tony's thirty-third birthday four years earlier. He lay as if sleeping, his hands folded on his chest, his body warm, his beautiful face radiant in the light of the flickering candles. I don't know how long I stayed there with him after his heart stopped beating, gazing at him, caressing him, trying to memorize the impressions of my eyes and fingers. I never thought I would want to touch a dead body. Now I didn't want to let one go.

Finally, I made myself get up and call the funeral home. Five minutes later, their van pulled up in front of the house. I let them in with their rolling cart and plastic sheets, then fled to the backyard, unable to watch them take his body away. When one of them came out to tell me it was over, I somehow found my way to the phone and called our friends, our same old friends for all these years. They came over and sat with me around the kitchen table long into the night. We finished Tony's bottle of wine and several more.

Along with the waves of grief that flooded through me, the unbearable, uncontrollable sense of loss, I felt something else— an unexpected pride. Tony had made some bad decisions in the ten years he lived with AIDS. There were times when he was weak, times when he was selfish, times when he embraced the victim role with a vengeance. I knew with absolute clarity that his death was not one of those times. He had made his choice; he had executed it with consideration and sureness. Finally, he was not a victim anymore.

In the morning, I went to the neighbor's house where my sons were playing and told those two little boys their daddy had died. Vincie burst into tears the second I said the words. Hayes held back for a while. I asked if they wanted to see his body and they did, so I took them to the funeral home and they saw. They saw that that body was not really Tony anymore. They drew pictures for him and tucked them, along with the photos of themselves I had in my wallet, into the blankets around his body. I took them into the chapel and tried to explain what I knew of how to pray.

At home, I dragged out the cedar chest and read them the letters Tony had written, full of reminiscences and reassurances that he would always be with them. "Take good care of Mommy and make sure she's okay and please always give her a special little kiss and tell her it's from her Big Beau Angel," he wrote to Vincie. "If you play any sports, please be careful and try not to get too banged up, I don't think Mommy's nerves could take it." In each letter, he writes angrily of AIDS, of his hope that "by the time you are big boys, they will find a cure for this stupid disease."

After that, we watched the video a friend had made, a montage of pictures and home video of Tony with an Annie Lennox soundtrack. It showed him in his first communion outfit, his high school graduation robe, in a blue sweatsuit with all of his skating trophies. Grinning in his rose garden, all dressed up to go out with me and Nancy and Steve, standing with Hayes on a balcony overlooking Florence.

It was the scene of him playing with the boys in the pool, the

first summer Vince could swim, when finally Hayes started crying and we all cried together.

On Monday morning, the obituary appeared in the paper,
and Hayes asked if we could bring it with us when he went to
school. Tony had died right after the first week of first grade, and
I thought if Hayes seemed up to it, it would be best for him to
get settled in a routine instead of missing school.

The teacher, the principal, and the school counselor gathered
Hayes's new classmates in a circle on the floor and explained that
something very sad and unusual had happened—Hayes's daddy
had died. Some of the little girls started to cry. Others had questions. Hayes leaned against me and listened as the adults answered them.

He asked me to read the obituary out loud, which I did, and
then his teacher tacked it up on the bulletin board. It stayed
there all year long. She told me many times Hayes would go up
to the board and stand there for a moment, gazing at his father's
smiling face.

Months later, I told the boys the whole truth about their
father's death. At first, they didn't believe what I was telling
them.

That's not how Daddy died, said Vincie. He just died.

No, Vince, he took the pills, like I said.

He shouldn't have done that, said Hayes.

But, Hayes, remember how sick he was? Remember how he
couldn't have fun anymore and he hurt all the time? It was just
going to get worse and worse. Soon we would have gone to visit
him and he wouldn't even have recognized us.

They still looked disbelieving, so I went on. Soon, he
wouldn't have been able to get out of bed at all. He would have
had to eat through tubes. He would have had to wear diapers.

Diapers? they repeated in unison, incredulous, struggling not to giggle.

Yes, diapers.

Oh God, said Hayes. No wonder.

According to Tony's instructions, his memorial service was held on top of Mount Bonnell overlooking Lake Austin, in the same spot where we'd gathered to say goodbye to Peewee seven years before. He had made lists of who would speak, who would sing, who would light candles, ordered helium balloons in Mardi Gras colors for the kids to release at the end. I would read that old poem of mine he liked, everyone would hold hands in a circle, afterward we would go back to the house for Philly cheese steaks and get very drunk.

About a hundred and fifty people came to the memorial gathering, friends and neighbors and coworkers and hair clients and several dozen children, all the kids who'd played games with him and gone swimming with him and had their hair cut by him, who'd been comforted by him when they woke in the night during a sleepover. They stood in a circle within the grown-ups' larger one, clutching their purple, green, and yellow balloons, and no one let theirs go by accident before the very end.

PERSISTENCE OF MEMORY

A couple of months after Tony died, I was driving the kids to school and "Modern Love" came on the radio, the old David Bowie song that was so popular the year we met. As has become almost inevitable when I listen to the radio, I started crying—whole decades of popular music do this to me now. Commercials do this to me, cemeteries, beauty salons, getting a massage, not getting a massage, tall, thin men, men with wire-rimmed glasses, billboards for Newport 100s, waking up in the middle of the night, trying to pick a movie to rent, the list goes on.

Vincie, already familiar with the phenomenon, asked, Does this song remind you of Daddy?

Yes, I told him, this was one of our favorite songs.

Don't you think it's still one of his favorite songs? asked Vince.

Oh, Vincie, I don't know, I answered, holding back a sob of frustration. I don't even know if they have music in heaven.

Well, why don't we open the windows? he suggested.

Do what?

Open the windows, so Daddy can hear it in heaven.

They believe what Tony wrote in the letters he left for them—that he is in heaven; he might even be an angel with wings. He can look down and see them and hear them; he is with them all the time. It's amazing watching children deal with death—both the innocence of their faith and the straightforwardness of their grief when faith escapes them. One night, Hayes couldn't sleep; I heard him in there whimpering, and when I went in, he said, I can't remember Tony. He's started to do that, call him Tony instead of Daddy.

Oh, I knew exactly what he meant. Time passes, months and months now. He slips so surely away from us. He is really and truly not coming back. You want to say, Ollie, ollie in free, okay, come on out now, we're sick of this. But more and more surely, the immediacy escapes you; the last time he walked in that door was a long time ago. He fades into memory, into family legend, into the words we use to tell the stories. But "fade" is too gentle; it is painful and harsh, like having a tooth pulled, you feel those last threads of flesh stretching and snapping and then all you can think of is the hole in your mouth.

A couple of years ago, I was on a plane to New York reading an article in *Texas Monthly* about a family that had suffered terribly from AIDS. It had started with blood transfusions and then was transferred from each of the brothers to their wives. The part that struck me most was when the ten-year old boy, who had AIDS himself and whose mother had already died, was flying a kite one day with his grandmother, one of the only uninfected members of the family, when the wind whipped the string out of his hands. The grandmother and the reporter were stricken, but the little boy took it calmly.

Don't worry. Mom will catch it for us, he said.

I was reading along and I burst into tears. *Mom will catch it for us.* I talked about the article for months without quite admitting why, trying to hear the clear bell tolling and not flinch.

When Vincie said to turn up the radio that day, I had a sense of déjà vu. It was the kite, I finally realized, the kite I wept over so many times. For so many years, I lived with a combination of dread and disbelief, but I could not experience both at the same time. I could not imagine Tony's death; I could not escape it; I could not have these two thoughts at once. Those parallel tracks

were not only internal; our life had this mixture of great and terrible, of happy denial and despairing acceptance. We lived a good
day as if a horrible yesterday and an unknown tomorrow did not
exist. This sounds reasonable in principle, but it's schizophrenic,
fragile, brittle. You leave the scene of the crime the second it's
over and you never clean up the blood and it happens again and
again and soon you are living in a very small room because there
is blood all over the rest of the house.

It is a vertiginous feeling, trying to reconstruct the past, real-
izing how much my memories have been revised to fit my later
understandings of and rationalizations for what happened. If
something doesn't fit the story, it just gets left out. Until it
sneaks back one day, suddenly appears amid the other memories, and the simple narrative line is wrecked, the neat explanation no longer works. If there is a truth at all in this world of
overlapping subjectivities, it sometimes seems too complicated
to hold in my head.

I wish so much sometimes he could come back and tell me
everything, fill in all the blanks, exactly what happened and
when and why, and I could tell him that I found the morphine
pills I thought he'd taken behind my back that last time in New
Jersey and I'm so sorry I didn't believe him when he was telling
the truth. I think maybe we could be straight with each other
now. I know he would want me to get this right.

If Tony were alive, we would have been married almost ten
years now, except if Tony were alive, I suppose we would not be
married anymore. By the time he died, I had almost forgotten
how much I loved him and where that love came from. How
much fun we had. What a good-natured and considerate and
dear person he was. Tony always said that he loved me uncondi-

tionally. I believe that he did. Our love for each other grew dark and twisted and even hollow, but it never went away; perhaps that was part of our curse. Love came first, and last, and stuck with us, stubborn and battered, through all the storms in between. Now that I don't have to fight anymore, I can feel that love in its fullness again, and the bewilderment over and over: how can it be that he is gone?

And then sometimes when I am taking a walk or playing with the boys or eating something delicious, I feel a greediness of being alive, not dead, a survivor's half-guilty joy. To see the sky and the trees, to feel the warmth of the sun and the strength of my muscles, simply to wake up, to get dressed, to move and to breathe: I would not give those things up. And it reminds me of when I realized that even those very basic things, the sight of the sky in the morning, meant nothing to Tony anymore. What AIDS did not take from him, he finally gave away, living from morphine shot to morphine shot, from cigarette to cigarette, waiting for the end.

But there is no end, no end in my heart. This afternoon when I was driving the boys home from school, that old song "Alive and Kicking" came on the radio. Tony and I argued about the band Simple Minds for years. At first, I hated them—I called them the Stupid Fools—but he converted me as he did in so many matters of taste, and I became such a fanatic he probably wished he hadn't. I am thinking all this as the song is playing, and I feel Hayes and Vincie watching me.

I turn to look at my beautiful sons, each with his father's sandy hair and long legs. They know what I'm thinking. I know what they're thinking too.

So I roll down the window and turn the radio up.

Acknowledgments

I am deeply indebted to the following people and institutions for their assistance in the writing of this book:

Tony Winik, who read pages and gave encouragement for as long as he could.

Robin Desser, my editor, with whom I also fell in love at first sight, and whose contribution to this project has been incalculable.

Patricia Van der Leun, my agent, co-conspirator, and beloved friend.

Robb Walsh, critic, cheerleader, lifesaver, head cook.

Audience #1: Jane Winik, Nancy Winik Cerbo Nalewaiski, Naomi Shihab Nye, Ken Blair, Judith Munyon, Jim and Jessica Shahin, Liz Lambert and Margaret Tucker, Anita Tschurr, Pete LaBonne and Shelley Valachovic, Scott and Lexanne Van Osdol, Mark Dean, Francisco Goldman, Sandye Renz, Frank and Debbie Heubach, Jo Ann Schmidt, Robin Bradford, Judy Frels, Robert Draper, Polly Brannan, Sue Weiner, and the late Phil Born, one of the best readers who ever lived.

The family, friends, and neighbors who have helped me take care of my sons this past year, particularly Grace and Rodney Fell, Dave Walsh, Mitzi Markese, Tomi and Dan Dominguez,

Lindsey Thompson and Bill Thompson, Dana Ellinger, Tom and Gael Mallouk, and, again, Jim and Jessica Shahin.

The Flight of the Mind women's writing workshop in Oregon, The Hambidge Center in Georgia, and the writers and artists I got to know at each place, particularly Grace Paley, who gave me a big push in the right direction.

ABOUT THE AUTHOR

Marion Winik is heard regularly on National Public Radio's "All Things Considered." Her essays have appeared in *Parenting, Redbook, Glamour, Cosmopolitan, The Los Angeles Times, Texas Monthly,* and *The Utne Reader,* among other publications. She is the author of *Telling.* She lives in Austin, Texas, with her two sons.